ENKINDLE

REVIVING THE CHURCH FROM WITHIN

K. KALE YU

ELMORETOWNES

Enkindle: Reviving the Church from Within

Elmore Townes Publishing

First Edition: April 2026

In referencing biblical passages, the New Revised Standard Version (NRSV) is used throughout, unless otherwise noted.

ISBN: 979-8-9926540-7-3

Printed in the United States of America

For Enkindled Souls

Contents

Introduction

Few could have predicted that *Who Moved My Cheese?* (1998)—a simple book about little humans and mazes—would become a worldwide phenomenon.[1] The book is a huge success, with forty-six million copies printed in forty-seven languages. Not only did business schools start using the book in their courses, but multinational corporations also began organizing meetings and training events centered around its main message. High-level executives at companies like General Electric, Procter & Gamble, and Hewlett-Packard recommended the book to their management teams, while Southwest Airlines went a step further by purchasing a copy for every single one of its 27,000 workers.[2]

The main storyline stays very simple from start to finish, but it's actually a clever way to teach some big life lessons. The story unfolds through the experience of four small residents: two mice named Sniff and Scurry, and two little humans called Hem and Haw. Every day, they go into the maze, tirelessly inspecting the maze's interior in search of cheese. By paying close attention to where they are, they cross out old routes to ensure they explore somewhere new. One day, their search finally leads them to Cheese Station C, where they find a room overflowing with cheese. Never before had they seen so much cheese. They are thrilled beyond belief.

Over time, they settle into a rhythm, taking the same route, arriving at the same spot at the same time every single morning. At first, they ran. Then they trotted. They now slow-walk through the maze as they've memorized every twist and turn. Their alertness and vigilance fade. It takes them much longer to move or respond to what is happening. In time, the incredible feeling of discovering a mountain of cheese vanishes and is replaced by an assumption that their supply of cheese will never run out, believing that nothing bad could ever happen to them. No longer feeling a sense of urgency, they stay in bed longer, and then head out for a leisurely walk instead of keenly tracking their steps like they did in the past.

Even though the world around them has changed, Hem and Haw stay exactly where they are. It never crosses their minds that their cheese will never be there for them. Not so with Sniff and Scurry, however. They aren't just eating; they're mindful of the fact that the big heap of cheese is shrinking even though it still looks like there is a lot of cheese left. On the other hand, Hem and Haw ignore any signs of trouble, feeling way too sure of themselves, but Sniff and Scurry are paying close attention and realize that their cheese—at some point in the future—will disappear.

That day finally comes. They enter the room only to discover—much to their shock and horror—that there is no cheese. The whole room is completely bare, not even a little bit was left. Hem and Haw are in disbelief, standing there like two statues. In contrast, Sniff and Scurry took one look and immediately got ready to roll. The two humans curiously watched Sniff and Scurry slip on their running shoes and dash out into the maze to find more cheese.

Instead of moving on, Hem and Haw remain in shock, but the feeling of confusion slowly turns into anger as they demand to know where their cheese went. "Who moved my cheese?" they shouted. They cannot believe that anyone would be so mean. They yell, "It's not fair!" They return to Cheese Station C every morning in the fanciful hope that someone will return their cheese, but they end up feeling just as frustrated and disappointed as the last. They are in a rut, doing the same things over and over, with no improvement to their situation. Instead of looking for a solution, they sit around and relive the good old days when their lives were easy and the cheese was plentiful.

Similarly, many churches find themselves in this same position. The traditional source of supply they once relied on is very low, or near exhaustion. Even while they feel a deep uncertainty about their survival, church leaders fall back on the familiar. It feels safer to stick with what they know than to risk the uncertainty of something new. Many hope things will go back to the way they were. They hold out for a return to the normal that keeps them from making the changes necessary to survive.

The High-Water Mark of Church

Never before had American churches seen such a massive supply as they did during the years following World War II. More people went to church than at any other time in US history as churchgoing became an important part of the American way of life in the postwar era. In 1954, *Time* magazine claimed, "Today the Christian faith is back in the center of things."[3]

One of the striking facts of this era is that church membership grew at a faster rate than the US population, "from 57 percent of the US population in 1950 to 63.3 percent in 1960."[4] This development is even more impressive when you remember that it happened during the era of the baby boomers, a time when the population was skyrocketing. Birth rates soared, the economy boomed, and the single-family home in the suburbs became the American dream.

Since the public strongly supported churchgoing, the vigorous pursuit of evangelism and church growth wasn't necessary. Back then, the harvest was plentiful, especially in the newly created suburbs on the outskirts of towns and cities. After studying population trends, new churches were strategically placed to follow the shifting demographics. In *The Fifties Spiritual Marketplace: American Religion in a Decade of Conflict*, Robert Ellwood writes, "It was the U.S. denominational society in action."[5] The incredible surge in the number of new churches reflects, according to Ellwood, the "supply side paradigm for religious participation."[6]

Church membership grew so consistently that people believed that the high numbers would only continue. Throughout the vast majority of the 1950s and the 1960s, more than seven out of every ten people in the United States were members of a local church.[7] To put those numbers into perspective, it means that if you walked down Main Street, over two-thirds of the people you met were members of a congregation.

Churches became a natural gathering place for residents in the area. As community hubs, churches were where neighbors connected, shared lives, and shaped their future together. In his seminal book, *Protestant–Catholic–Jew*, Will Herberg describes the religiousness of the era as "a way of sociability of 'belonging' rather a way of reorienting life to God."[8] On the community calendar, the church offered a wide range of seasonal events, family-focused fun, special performances, and community suppers.

The entire sanctuary was overflowing with people from the front to the back. On special Sundays, additional folding chairs were necessary in the aisles to accommodate all the extra people. Some had to expand their main worship area to account for the crowds. Because so many children were coming to Sunday school, churches had to add a brand-new wing to the building.

Faith was at a high point. Nearly half of the American population attended church in the late 1950s, which was "the highest percentage in U.S. history."[9] It was as if a huge mountain of cheese appeared, but it wasn't long before that mountain started to get smaller and smaller. The church started to get quieter over time. The long pews weren't as crowded as before. Fewer children were running around the hallways. As of 2024, the percentage of adults who go to church on a regular basis dropped to 30 percent, and there is no sign that this will reverse anytime soon.[10]

Haw's Awakening

With no cheese, Hem and Haw sat in the empty room and clung to the fond memories of the past, recalling the mountain of cheese that they enjoyed so much. However, replaying trips down memory lane isn't a substitute for real food, and their hunger grew with every passing day. It was a sudden spark of insight that eventually woke Haw up to the truth. Perhaps, Haw thought, Sniff and Scurry were right. Believing the mice might be onto something, Haw relays this insight to Hem who was offended by the thought. "What would they know?" Hem quickly dismisses the idea. "They're just mice ... we're smarter than mice," he says. With a sense of pride, Hem adds, "We're Little people ... we should be able to figure this out."

As the days turned into weeks, the two humans, who used to be quite heavy because of the overabundance of food, eventually grew thinner and thinner as they waited for cheese that never returned. Haw finally loses his patience and shouts, "Let's go!" but Hem insists on staying put. He says, "No ... I like it here. It's comfortable. It's what I know. Besides it's dangerous out there." Haw reminded Hem that they once traveled widely through the corridors and sections before they found the station, but that wasn't enough for Hem to overcome his fears. "I'm getting too old for that," Hem says, "and I'm afraid I'm not interested in getting lost and making a fool of myself. Are you?"

As the hunger became harder to ignore, Haw suddenly broke out in laughter because he finally saw how funny and pathetic their situation had become, waiting and expecting the cheese to somehow reappear out of nowhere. He saw how foolish they were, simply because they were afraid to move. Haw understands now that the cheese will not reappear; instead, he knows he must go to the cheese. The breakthrough came when he understood that he wasn't entitled to the cheese; the cheese simply exists in a new, unfamiliar location where individuals need to go find it.

Haw tries to convince his friend that staying is useless, but Hem is having none of it. His fears keep him hostage, as the thought of entering the unknown parts of the maze overwhelms him. When Hem realizes that Haw is serious about leaving, he tries to persuade him to stay: "Why don't you just wait with me—they'll put the cheese back?" Haw reluctantly stays but not for long. Within days, he realizes it's pointless and decides to move on. Before venturing out, Haw writes on the wall, in big letters so that Hem can't miss it: "If You Do Not Change, You Can Become Extinct."

In Search of New Church Members

Enkindle is about finding new cheese, that is, church members; however, like trying to find new cheese in the maze, the road ahead will test our resolve. Even though church leaders are working as hard as possible to make things happen, they often face big hurdles, particularly a way of thinking that blocks new ideas from gaining traction. For Hem and Haw, they held on tight to the mistaken belief that things ought to remain just like they always were. Since they couldn't understand the truth of their problem, the confusion kept them from taking the necessary steps to save themselves.

In the same way, a lot of congregations find a sense of security in their long-standing traditions and prefer to remain with what they know rather than take a risk on unfamiliar approaches. Some feel they need to preserve their church identity from innovations that may upend the way things have been done, as if adopting them is like betraying the very people who founded it. If you try to pitch something that breaks away from the usual routine, you might hear that phrase that emphasizes the way things are: "We've never done it that way," (or its closely related cousin, "We've always done it this way.") When we insist on the way things are, we lose the flexible quality that is necessary to visualize new and exciting opportunities.

As the number of people attending keeps dropping and the need to do something becomes more urgent, congregations are convinced that if they just do their old programs better and stronger, the people will come back. Unfortunately, they are not coming back. We are standing at a crossroads where more churches are at risk of closure than in any previous generation. Lovett Weems uses the phrase "the coming death tsunami" to describe the wave of deaths that will happen as the baby boomer generation gets older and passes away. A very significant portion of the annual giving depends on the support of older members who are seventy and above. The death tsunami, Weems warns, is a mathematical certainty. Weems makes a heartfelt appeal, knowing that the window of opportunity is closing fast. "The time to make choices is now—while there are still choices to make. Otherwise, circumstances will very likely make the choices for us in the future."[11] It is no longer a question of *if* churches will close, but *how fast.*

While it's true that the average age of church members is getting older, there are evolving social undercurrents that present additional risks. For example, trust used to be the glue that held society together. Over the past decades, however, the level of confidence that the general public has in religious and social institutions has fallen to an all-time low, especially for members of Gen Z (those born 1997–2012) who have the lowest level of trust. A recent study found that "a staggering" percentage of young people rate their trust in religious institutions at five or below on a ten-point scale.[12] The natural reaction is to pull back from institutions, including the church, and we are seeing this development. A recent Gallup report from 2024 shows that the number of people regularly going to church keeps going down. Based on the current trends, Gallup predicts that "church attendance will likely continue to decline in the future, given younger Americans' weaker attachments to religion."[13]

Enkindle offers a way to reverse church decline, but not in the way you might expect. Most people think the key to reviving a struggling church is finding a successful program or innovative activity that will convince people to join the church. When people talk about evangelism or outreach or reaching the neighborhood, the main focus is usually on how many new people they can bring to church. We believe that by offering contextualized programs for every age group, we can attract families.

This vision of strategic expansion is so deeply ingrained in the way we think about church growth that we rarely consider other ways. Examples of strategic programs include modernizing worship styles, launching new community models, following denominational initiatives, or imitating the successes of larger churches. Even when a church attempts to do something that is brand-new or modern, it also feels very familiar. We see a recurring pattern of defining the desired outcome and the series of steps to achieve it.

Elizabethtown United Methodist Church's approach typifies how many churches try to reverse their decline. With membership in steady decline, Elizabethtown UMC in Ohio faced the very real prospect of permanent closure. To address the lack of families in the pews, the church expanded its community outreach. Dennis Simpson, who has been a member of

Elizabethtown for sixty-nine years, told a local news station, "We brought in new music, we've had activities every month, we've had movie night, we've had a large trunk or treat activity with as many as 200 kids showing up for that."[14] However, attendance remained stagnant, with only about a dozen people in the pews each week. Meanwhile, rising upkeep costs for the aging, historic building made it clear they were fighting a losing battle. After more than two hundred years of ministry in the greater Cincinnati area, they made the hard decision to close in 2025. "It's sad," Simpson said, "but it's probably for the best."

Enkindle offers a different way to think about church revitalization. Instead of chasing the next church initiative, this approach finds the spark of renewal where it has always been: with the people in the pews. The freestyle approach awakens leaders to see their members as the true engines of church growth. Church leaders look to their own people—not outside programs—for authentic ministry ideas.

The Holy Spirit enkindles a holy fire within the hearts of the people. By empowering Spirit-led initiatives from their own members, congregations release a truly transformative power. As regular church people are enkindled, their dormant gifts emerge, and their faith grows as they live out their calling. A local church can thrive on the authentic leadership of everyday people, but every church and every member will yield a different result because enkindling focuses on the individual and each person brings their unique self to the process. An enkindled church culture moves away from prepackaged solutions, focusing instead on identifying and releasing the unique ministry ideas of its own members.

The possibilities are boundless. The regular members in local churches, from children to seniors, are often an untapped source of ministry inspiration. Freestyle focuses on the powerful, grassroots witness of ordinary people who are local experts within their own communities and subcultures. When ordinary people, enkindled by the Holy Spirit, step up, their authenticity organically attracts those outside the church.

Enkindle

In a moment of mentorship, Paul urged Timothy to fan the flame to keep his inner fire burning bright. During our most discouraging and lonely seasons, we must guard our faith-flame and turn to God to reignite our weary souls. Paul writes: "I remind you to rekindle the gift of God that is within you" (2 Timothy 1:6). The original Greek word used for "rekindle" in the passage literally means to "kindle afresh" or "keep in full flame."

Paul's exhortation to Timothy is a reminder that spiritual fire doesn't keep itself going; the fire requires tending and maintenance to keep the zeal of the Lord from fading. Paul is concerned that Timothy's embers have been dimmed and encourages him to stir up and reawaken his enthusiasm for the Lord. The term *rekindle* is an apt translation of the Greek word that has "fire" (πῦρ or *pur*) as its base, root word.[15] *Pur* is the root for many English words related to fire, such as pyre, pyrotechnics, and pyrogenic. Paul's words remind us that a flickering spark, enkindled within an individual, can transform into a blazing fire.

This book's title, *Enkindle*, sounds similar to the word "kindle," and both share the core meaning of ignite, but "enkindle" delivers a more potent punch. "Enkindle" is a stronger version of "kindle," as the prefix "en–" is an intensive prefix, that adds "to put in" or "to cause to be" to the meaning of the word. The combination specifically stresses the action of setting something ablaze, either physically or metaphorically. Used in a literary context, "enkindle" marks the start of a powerful process or emotion and describes an arousal of passions, hope, love, zeal, or even conflict. One could, for example, enkindle a forgotten love for life; enkindle the start of reconciliation in a fractured family; or enkindle a sudden awareness to fight for survival.

In church liturgy, the phrase "Enkindle in us the fire of Your love" serves as a petition within the invocation of the Holy Spirit (also known as the *Veni Sancte Spiritus*), a prayer used to invite holy presence before meetings, classes, or worship. "Enkindle" is used in many hymns as a metaphor for the internal sparking of spiritual vitality. In Isaac Watts's "Come, Holy Spirit, Heavenly Dove," he asks the Holy Spirit to "enkindle a flame of sacred love" in "cold hearts." Similarly, the ancient "Holy Spirit, Lord of Light" uses the term to represent an intimate, God-infused indwelling, petitioning the Spirit to "enkindle in our hearts the fire of Thy love." In "Spirit of Faith, Come Down," Charles Wesley expands this usage by evoking the intensity of the Pentecost as he prays to "enkindle the baptismal fire," while in "Love Divine, All Loves Excelling," it asks God to "enkindle every trembling heart" as an act of emboldening and comforting believers.

Once the Holy Spirit ignites a fire, the combustion within the person demands the release of its pressurized energy. The individual, as a result, is propelled out of passive faith and into a life of purpose, driven by a Spirit-led urge to leave a mark on the world around them. In the freestyle approach to church growth, the burden of revitalizing a struggling congregation shifts away from a ministry program and falls squarely on the Holy Spirit. In the Pentecost narrative in Acts 2, the disciples were "filled with the Holy Spirit" and, as a result, went out into the streets of Jerusalem to proclaim Christ. Peter gave an impassioned, God-inspired message that stirred the hearts of the people who then asked, "What should we do?" (Acts 2:37). Peter replied, "Repent, and be baptized every one of you in the name of Jesus Christ so that your sins may be forgiven; and you will receive the gift of the Holy Spirit" (v. 38). About "three thousand" people received Christ and came forward to be baptized "that day" (v. 41).

Local churches are the ideal environment for enkindled souls to launch their grassroots initiatives. However, the question remains: Can a local congregation pivot from "the way we've always done it" to empower something entirely new? Innovation is messy. Friction is bound to happen when new fires meet old structures. Enkindled souls rarely fit neatly into traditional patterns. However, they bring a contagious excitement and energy to their mission. When a church celebrates and releases these souls, a ripple effect begins: Others find their own inspiration by witnessing the light. When the disciples spilled out into the streets of Jerusalem, they created such a messy scene that the crowds were left "bewildered" (Acts 2:6) and "perplexed" (v. 12). Some onlookers reacted with "sneers," accusing them of being drunk (v. 13).

The unexpected and spontaneous nature of the Holy Spirit can unsettle people in the church, especially if they prize formality, routine, and precedent. Innovative, untested, ideas rarely fit the mold of what people expect from church life. At the same time, when our people are stretched thin, they often miss the fresh excitement the Holy Spirit is stirring up. In his letter to the

Ephesians, Paul urges them to expand their capacity to recognize God's movement: "The power at work within us is able to accomplish abundantly far more than all we can ask or imagine" (Ephesians 3:20). The same verse in *The Message* reads: "God can do anything, you know—far more than you could ever imagine or guess or request in your wildest dreams!"

To truly support enkindled souls, a congregation must be willing to step out of its comfort zone and into the unknown. The Holy Spirit is rarely predictable, and revival may well begin with the youngest members of the congregation. In Luke 10:21, Jesus "rejoiced in the Holy Spirit and said, 'I thank you, Father, Lord of heaven and earth, because you have hidden these things from the wise and the intelligent and have revealed them to infants; yes, Father, for such was your gracious will.'"

Enkindling Laypeople

Building on the themes of *Freestyle: Evangelism as Expressing Jesus* (2025), this book explores how enkindled laypeople can reverse church decline.[16] The opening chapters analyze the state of the church today—a situation many describe as a crisis. Statistical trends reveal a church facing immense pressure to stay relevant as many congregations teeter on the brink of closure. While churches work hard to halt their decline, they often rely on outdated models that no longer resonate. Churches aren't just struggling for members; they are also overlooking the very people who could reverse the decline: their own members. While churches respect laypeople as indispensable volunteers, they seldom see them as drivers of church revitalization.

The book rejects the idea that everyday members aren't qualified to innovate their own outreach and lead the way in renewal. What if the architects of church growth were regular members rather than outside experts? Instead of following an external method, imagine church members creating the very outreach that sparks their congregation's growth.

This book shows that lacking a pastoral title is a hidden strength; everyday people build more genuine bonds because they connect as peers rather than religious authorities. Living and working alongside their neighbors gives church members a deep, intuitive understanding of local life—an insider's view that an outside expert could never match. Because they share a common vocabulary and culture, their message has a natural relatability that no official church program can replicate. A native understanding is their superpower; it lets enkindled souls reach deep into subcultures that are otherwise impenetrable.

Building an enkindled culture is less about creating new programs and more about trusting the Holy Spirit—letting people freestyle their own ministry without imposing our own desired outcomes or preset procedures. Traditional evangelism models often come with execution models like contextualization, small groups, third space, or new missional communities. In an enkindled culture, they are not asked to follow a plan; they are asked to follow the Holy Spirit and create their own plan. True excitement takes hold when people own *their* mission—and that only happens when they are free to freestyle their own Spirit-led innovation without a hidden agenda.

How does an enkindled soul breathe life into a dying church? From a freestyle perspective, a church doesn't grow because it tries to grow; growth is the unintended by-product of a Spirit-led life that spills out into the neighborhood. It's church growth without trying to grow the church. When a congregation is Spirit-led, the visible joy of its members becomes an irresistible magnet for those outside its walls.

It's the realness of the people that draws outsiders in, not how well the program is executed. Staged events can feel preplanned, detached, and impersonal, but the unrehearsed excitement of people is what connects the listener to the message. As a result, a congregation grows naturally through connections that feel organic rather than manufactured or forced. An enkindled culture thrives on the spontaneity of the Holy Spirit's will.

This is where people have trouble: letting go of control to let the Holy Spirit lead. Admittedly, the Spirit's guidance isn't always clear: It can move us into a season of waiting just as fast as a season of action. Depending on your view, the Spirit's spontaneity is either thrilling or exhausting. In John 3, Jesus left Nicodemus baffled. The spiritual metaphors were lost on Nicodemus who asked, "What do you mean?" (John 3:4, NLT). Jesus replies, "The wind blows where it chooses, and you hear the sound of it, but you do not know where it comes from or where it goes. So it is with everyone who is born of the Spirit" (John 3:8).

In the upcoming chapters, we'll meet people from all walks of life, each representing different generations, callings, and communities. A community isn't defined by its walls, but by the shared values and goals that bring people together. These communities provide belonging and identity, proving that everyday people carry a powerful message to their own circles. Chapter 5 focuses on how everyone is an expert in their own way, from a young child and a high school cafeteria worker to a self-described "LEGO nerd." Though none are experts in a traditional sense, they possess a deep, lived-in knowledge of their own communities. Subcultures are everywhere in our modern world, and we often find ourselves moving between several of them every day. The best missionaries aren't outsiders brought in for the job—they are the people already living within that subculture.

In chapter 6, we see how the Holy Spirit's fire shifts our identity toward a future-focused, Jesus-centered vision. The term enkindling suggests that something is already there—a passion, a yearning, or an unresolved knot—waiting for a spark to catch. But even enkindled people have their doubts: "What if I'm wrong?" or "What if I fail?" This is where the local church can reposition itself as a welcoming place that helps enkindled souls discern their call and actively support their journey. In doing so, they become partners in the Holy Spirit's work.

To walk in step with the Spirit, a congregation must cultivate a courageous openness—moving beyond rigid formats to embrace the untapped potential of everyday people and the unpredictable possibilities of God. To give people the freedom to follow the Spirit is to trust an unscripted outcome. Choosing to let the Spirit lead can feel like a walk through the fog, but it's in the mist where we hold the Lord's hand the tightest. While human-designed programs offer order, only the Spirit brings the kind of heart-transforming renewal that genuinely stirs people to seek more.

1

Present-Day Church

In 2024, leaders at First Baptist Church in Mount Vernon broke the news: The budget shortfall was insurmountable, and the church would have to close. Though they'd seen the budget shrink for years, the reality was still a shock. Members had fought to keep the doors open, but they couldn't stop the slow bleed of dwindling offerings, passing members, and young families moving away from their small town east of St. Louis.

For the people at First Baptist, the end felt inevitable—not a matter of *if*, but *when*. It hadn't always been this way. Decades ago, the church overflowed with life. Longtime members still remember they had to "install movable dividers in the fellowship hall" just to make room for all the children and adults.[17] First Baptist Church transitioned from a peak in the 1960s with over six hundred members to a final, struggling congregation of fewer than twenty, leaving a fourteen-thousand-square-foot sanctuary largely empty. The massive building, once a symbol of pride, became an unsustainable financial burden, with winter heating costs exceeding the pastor's salary.

There was little argument against the closure, but a profound sense that they were losing a piece of themselves. For over a century and a half, First Baptist had been woven into the fabric of Mount Vernon—a steady anchor for generations. Pastor Ryan Burge could not help but think about the sacrifices of the "countless members" who had contributed their time, labor, and money to build First Baptist. "They had," Burge writes, "given over and above their tithe to finance the bricks, the carpet and the pews."[18]

Churches Closing

In Oklahoma, another church, First United Methodist Church, was preparing to say goodbye. The details were far from ordinary: The person responsible for the closure was a product of the congregation itself. Derreck Belase, now the executive director for the Oklahoma Conference, faced the surreal task of shuttering the very church that had shaped him.

Belase made one final visit, taking in the sights and smells of the place that raised him. Located in the small town of Carnegie—named for the famed steel magnate—the church's roots actually predate Oklahoma's statehood. It started with a small group meeting in an old schoolhouse, long before the current walls were even built.

As the fourth generation of his family to call First United Methodist home, Belase felt the weight of that legacy. Looking out over the sanctuary, he could almost see his ancestors sitting in the very seats they had occupied for decades. "If I look back [to the back pews]," Belase says, "I could see my great-grandfather, Bud, and his brother, Doc, sitting a few rows back."[19] He felt himself drifting back into his childhood as memories began to play like a film. Even though he was only seven at the time, he still vividly remembered the 1984 bicentennial celebration "like it was yesterday."[20] The celebration began with the ringing of the new bell, a gift from the Scott family. Even now, Belase could visualize Eunice—Lois Scott's mother—using all her strength to excitedly ring the bell before the service.

Standing there in November, Belase couldn't help but remember the buzz that used to fill the church in anticipation for Christmas—a truly "magical time" for the congregation. The sanctuary underwent a makeover so dramatic it was unrecognizable. A massive tree touched the ceiling, covered in handmade Chrismons, while fresh greenery and glowing candles lined every wall.

The church was his second home, a place where his faith was carefully watched over and helped to grow. Though he had many different Sunday school teachers over the years, he "can remember all" of them. He especially loved Sunday evenings as a teen, eating pizza and Oreos in the church basement during youth meetings.

When the doctors broke the news of his father's cancer, the congregation rallied. They didn't just bring meals; they organized fundraisers and provided every kind of support they could manage. He still vividly remembers one Sunday when the entire church crowded around his father, laying on hands and praying for his recovery.

There are too many happy memories to count but "the main thing," Belase says, "I realized through my years in that church is just how much Jesus loves me. His followers taught and showed me his love." The seeds of his faith were planted in those pews long ago; after college, his church family wholeheartedly backed his decision to pursue ordination. As time passed, the pews grew emptier and emptier until there simply weren't enough people to keep the doors open.

Sitting in a familiar pew, Belase soaked in the moment with a heavy heart as First UMC held its final service on November 20, 2022. It had never crossed his mind that the church of his childhood would one day close—let alone that he would be the one in charge of its end. "My head can comprehend all this," Belase admits, "but my heart still breaks."[21]

A similar deep sadness hung over Ryan Burge as he presided over First Baptist's final service on July 21, 2024. In the final minutes of the service, Burge stood for the Benediction—the closing liturgical prayer that signaled the end of the service, and for the church itself. It marked the end of an era for First Baptist. He wondered if the end of First Baptist was a preview of what's to come for many more churches in the coming years. He writes, "I'm not sure if the church in

America will be there for the next generation like it was for me."[22]

Church in Free Fall

Ryan Burge's uncertainty about the church's future is grounded in research. As a social scientist and pastor, his latest work, *The Vanishing Church* (2026), explores the complex shifts happening across the religious landscape. The data reveals a harsh reality: The foundations of American church life are eroding faster than we imagined. The multigenerational bond of congregational life has fractured, as younger generations move away from the idea that preserving an institution is a requirement of faith. This loss of institutional loyalty has sent mainline Protestantism into "near free fall" as "the numbers of nonreligious [or 'nones'] were rising every single year."[23]

By 2030, an estimated 100,000 Protestant churches—nearly 20 percent—will shut their doors, according to sociologist and minister

Eileen Lindner.[24] This trend has accelerated significantly over the last decade. Ryan Burge agrees, estimating in a 2023 interview that a third of the country's 350,000 Christian congregations are now "on the brink of extinction."[25] No part of the country is immune, according to Burge. "We're going to see thousands of churches closing in America over the next 20 or 30 years in every part of the country, in every region and every state, urban, suburban, rural."[26]

These closures signal more than just empty buildings; they represent the fading of the values that once made the church the center of the community—a retreat from the moral and social values that once held church life together. A 2023 *Wall Street Journal* survey found that values "that helped define the national character for generations are receding in importance to Americans."[27] The decline of classic American traits is "so dramatic" that pollster Bill, who measured the survey, noted the results "paints a new and surprising portrait of a changing

America."[28] Back in 1998, seven out of ten (70%) people thought patriotism was "very important"; now, barely four out of ten (38%) do. Religion fared slightly better as 39 percent of those surveyed called religion "very important," compared to 62 percent in 1998.

The church once enjoyed a unique level of trust and respect that has since given way to skepticism. At a recent evangelism conference, I asked the audience to view the church through the eyes of a nonbeliever and try to imagine how they would think of the church today. While everyone agreed the church was more respected in their youth, they struggled to say the same for today.

The forum opened with a blunt assessment: "People think churchgoers are hypocrites." That sentiment set the tone for a wave of raw feedback. Attendees described a "skeptical and suspicious" public and a church culture that is "uncomfortable with change." The labels grew harsher as the session continued—"judgmental," "toxic," "not good enough," and "deeply divided."

One participant spoke for many when they mentioned feeling "rejected and hurt" by the very institution meant to welcome them. By the end, a cynical question from the back of the room summed up the mood: "What's the point? It makes no difference."

Given the multifaceted crisis weighing down on churches, the news that membership has fallen below 50 percent shouldn't come as a shock. It is a historic moment because, since Gallup first began tracking religious practices in 1937, church membership has never dropped this far. That year, Gallup measured church membership at 73%; it "remained near 70% for the next six decades, before beginning a steady decline around the turn of the 21st century."[29] Gallup has investigated whether the pandemic caused a temporary dip in 2020, but their research confirms that the decline is part of a much broader trend. According to Gallup, further decline in the coming decades seems "inevitable," given the "much lower levels of religiosity and church membership among younger versus older generations of adults."[30]

Clergy Burnout

For years, Daniel Whitehead dutifully carried out his role as pastor—feeding souls, building connections, and rushing from one meeting to the next. He didn't realize that the very vocation meant to offer spiritual sustenance to others was slowly draining his own passion, leaving him disconnected from himself and his family. Then, his wife made an observation that shook his world. She couldn't remember the last time she'd seen him smile. Her words struck hard, forcing a fresh and painful perspective on his life in ministry.

Whitehead saw that he had grown "numb" over the years. "I realized in that moment, it had been well over a year that I'd felt any emotion," he said. "No laughter, no tears, just numbness."[31] He was emotionally depleted, left without a map to guide his way forward. "I didn't have language, or self-permission, or a framework to really understand what I was going through," he recalled. It took a long pause before Whitehead could describe the void: "It was a feeling of fear, anxiety, and feeling trapped."

To recover, Whitehead had to untangle the stressors that had challenged his well-being. He realized he had been living in a state of "emotional overwhelm," his system constantly flooded by a schedule that had him running in circles. "[I was] moving from meeting to meeting," he recalled, "feeling the weight of people's expectations, having to be there for people when they're at their worst, and not really having an outlet to process that with."

Whitehead's experience is far from isolated; it reflects a national trend of occupational fatigue. Data from organizations like Barna and the Hartford Institute for Religion Research (HIRR) confirm that clergy burnout has reached a critical level. In a 2023 HIRR report, 44 percent of clergy admitted to seriously considering their current congregation—a figure that has more than doubled since 2021.[32] The crisis extends beyond individual congregations: 53 percent of clergy have now contemplated leaving the ministry altogether, up 16 percentage points from just two years prior. This vocational fatigue is hitting young leaders hardest. Barna's research highlights a startling generational divide: "One of the more alarming findings is that 46 percent of pastors under the age of 45 say they are considering quitting full-time ministry."[33] Barna warns: "Keeping the right younger leaders encouraged and in their ministry roles will be crucial to the next decade of congregational vitality in the U.S."

With the number of pastors reporting high job satisfaction plummeting from 72 percent in 2015 to just 52 percent in 2022, Barna CEO David Kinnaman warned that this trend signals "a crisis that the church has to address."[34] In 2015, a strong majority of pastors (72%) reported being "very satisfied" with their ministry work.[35] By late 2022, only 52 percent of pastors reported being "very satisfied"—a 20-point drop in just seven years. This vocational decline has left many carrying a heavy, silent burden of discouragement. Most alarming is the spike in burnout: Barna's research reveals that 40 percent of pastors are now at high risk, a nearly 400 percent increase from the 11 percent recorded in 2015.

In a 2022 op-ed, Anglican priest Tish H. Warren described the "overwhelming" fatigue of the modern pastor: "It was the relentless pace of issues, one after another. Everyone in their congregations seemed angry about different things, and everyone was looking to them to respond in the exact right way to that anger."[36] This pressure is compounded by a deteriorating sense of grace within the pews. Clergy are also grappling with a painful reality: The atmosphere of grace and respect that once defined the church has buckled under the weight of conflict, division, and hostility. Michael Keller, the pastor of Redeemer Lincoln Square, a Presbyterian church in New York City, summed up the situation when he said, "We've become less of a forgiving culture."[37]

The church is facing a double-edged sword: Society is becoming increasingly complex just as the clergy are reaching burnout at a higher rate. Pastors aren't just struggling to launch new initiatives in the face of decline; they are also managing a membership that has become far more vocal and demanding. The most frequent recommendation is a commitment to wellness boundaries—moving away from a culture of constant availability toward a more intentional schedule. By mindfully protecting time for personal replenishment, pastors can practice better stewardship of their own gifts. Ultimately, stepping back from relentless demands is not a sign of weakness, but a necessary strategy to sustain long-term ministry.

CLOSING THOUGHTS

Religious institutions are grappling with a hard reality: The framework for congregational vitality was designed for a cultural era that no longer exists. This has created a profound disconnect between the legacy church and the contemporary public. For the growing number of unchurched and unaffiliated, the modern church model often feels uninspiring and detached from the deep questions of daily life. A November 2025 Gallup report underscores this shift, revealing a 17-percentage-point drop in adults who view religion as important to their daily lives—from 66 percent in 2015 to 49 percent in 2025. This decline, according to Gallup, "ranks among the largest Gallup has recorded in any country over any 10-year period since 2007."[38]

Religion in America is undergoing a decentering, as the local congregation shifts from being the social glue of a community to a marginalized interest group. For decades, church attendance was an automatic habit; now that this link has been decoupled, congregations must prove their relevance to a skeptical public. "Fewer Americans," Gallup recently reported, "identify with a religion, church attendance and membership are declining, and religion holds a less important role in people's lives than it once did."[39] This shift is hitting churches where it hurts: The disappearance of volunteers now threatens various ministries and outreach projects, while dwindling pews inevitably lead to smaller and smaller budgets.

The American church is at a crossroads. The familiar patterns of the past are fading, making way for a new and yet-to-be-determined era of religious practice. This watershed moment demands a reimagining of evangelism that prioritizes authentic engagement over institutional maintenance. To navigate this change, the church must move away from a data-fixated focus on attendance and toward a deep commitment to its local community. The era of church as brand is giving way to a more natural movement where the focus is on the spontaneous, authentic experiences of everyday people enkindled by their faith.

2

Old and New Wineskins

Each December, Merriam-Webster selects the "Word of the Year" that reflects the collective anxieties of the previous twelve months. This choice serves as a barometer for the cultural mood, revealing our general outlook and deepest concerns. Before making a final decision, editors survey the linguistic landscape to identify the terms that made the greatest impact, eventually narrowing the field to a shortlist of finalists.

For 2023, the editors had a wealth of strong contenders; any one of them could have been a worthy choice. The shortlist featured both newly minted terms like "rizz" and "deepfake," alongside older words making a linguistic comeback, such as "dystopian" and "doppelganger." In the end, the editors bypassed technical terms and buzzworthy jargon in favor of a word that was familiar to everyone: "authentic."

Reflecting on their decision, the editors noted that "authentic" is "the term for something we're thinking about, writing about, aspiring to, and judging more than ever."[40] Although the word is ancient, its newfound relevance reveals a modern irony: We live in the most technologically advanced era in history, yet as AI and robots integrate into our daily routines, we feel more like strangers to one another, yearning for genuine connections.

According to Merriam-Webster, the uptick in people searching for the word's meaning was "substantial." It makes sense that "authentic" has gained such traction; as the line between real and fake becomes increasingly blurred, we find it harder to distinguish between the two. The more our lives are lived through screens, the more we crave genuine human connection. In a world of filtered images and performative thoughts, authenticity has become the most valuable currency for community building.

We have entered an era where the burden of verifying authenticity falls entirely on the individual. Sifting through the mental clutter of misleading content across multiple platforms can become an overwhelming task, forcing users into the role of constant fact-checkers. This leads to a heightened state of skepticism; we no longer move through the world passively, but with an investigative mindset. It is a protective posture— a questioning attitude that refuses to take things at face value. Increasingly, people are deciding for themselves what to believe, refusing to accept church teachings and directives without critical scrutiny.

The fact that terms like "deepfake" and "fake news" have seeped into our everyday language shows just how guarded we have become in an increasingly polarized environment. Everyone, it seems, is trying to sell us something. Churches are not exempt from this skepticism; a modern public can easily detect any lack of authenticity in evangelism or promotional campaigns. The era of the church as an untouchable social pillar has faded, and it is now scrutinized with the same questioning attitude applied to any other authority.

Scar Girl

While teaching a course on Religion in America at High Point University, I steered a conversation toward how social media affects faith. That naturally led us to the world of social media content creators.

"Can anyone be a social media influencer?" I asked the room.

"We have one here on campus," a student chimed in.

"Who?" I asked, my curiosity piqued.

"She goes by 'Scar Girl' on TikTok."

The atmosphere in the room suddenly shifted. The entire class perked up, and a strange tension filled the air—but I didn't know why. When I asked about her popularity, the answer shocked me: "She has nearly a million followers."

"A million? Really?" I was stunned and fascinated. I assumed she must possess some extraordinary talent to command such a massive following.

"So, what's her thing? Why is she so popular?"

"She has a scar on her face," a student said simply.

I was confused. "A scar? What's the big deal?"

"That's it," another student replied.

"That's *it*?" I pressed back.

It was then that the class realized their professor was entirely out of the loop.

"Well, there are also controversies," someone added.

"About her?"

"No," I was quickly corrected. "About the scar."

"About the *scar*? What's the controversy?"

"People think it's fake," someone explained. "That it's not a real scar and she's making it up."

As I struggled to figure out the fascination with Scar Girl, an emotionally charged debate erupted. Half the class insisted she was a fraud, while the other half vigorously defended her. I stood there, watching arguments and counterarguments fly. One student even claimed to know a friend of her roommate who never saw the scar.

Seeing the entire room engaged, I interjected: "Wait—do *all* of you know who Scar Girl is?"

Not only did everyone know Scar Girl, but a student went a step further to explain to me that she is like a celebrity and *everyone* on campus knows her.

At first, I couldn't take any of it seriously, a girl with a scar generating a million followers. But as I dug deeper, I realized the Scar Girl controversy exposed underlying anxieties that define Gen Z. It wasn't just a TikTok trend; it was an exercise in interactive engagement. Viewers don't just watch the videos; they become part of the story. The controversy begs the simple question: Is it real? She claims it's real but viewers are skeptical. This uncertainty creates tension, which in turn invites viewers into "authenticity police," who act as self-appointed detectives. They closely watch the videos for clues, weigh the merits of the case, and make a determination of her fakeness or realness based on their own analysis.

The audience doesn't just watch; they cross-check the findings of others, engage other followers, post thousands of comments, and create "stitch" videos (a compilation of video clips with commentary) to share (or debunk) theories. Acting like digital vigilantes, some even experimented with makeup to see if they could recreate the look—an effort to unmask the dark curved scar as manufactured deception. Even board-certified dermatologists chimed in with professional opinions on the scar. Meanwhile, Internet sleuths combed through her years of posts on other platforms, cross-referencing old photos to compare the color, shape, and exact position of the scar to expose any inconsistencies.

Scar Girl, however, maintained that the scar is very real—the result of an injury exacerbated by a chemical burn. Naysayers argued the scar was a very clever makeup trick designed to generate engagement and attract followers. Every time a viewer pointed out an inconsistency, she would post a rebuttal, creating a relentless back-and-forth between creator and audience. Yet, these responses would stir up new controversies that kept the story alive and gave followers fresh evidence to debate.

When a commenter demanded she rub the scar to prove it was real, Scar Girl did just that.

Yet the video failed to silence the skeptics; instead, it launched a new round of forensic analysis. Critics claimed the scrub was too light or the wipe too dry to remove professional-grade makeup. They accused her of deception and demanded definitive proof—even medical records—while her supporters jumped in to defend her, fighting as if the battle were their own. Viewers grew more emotionally invested in proving that the claims were either absolute truth or a total sham.

As I've learned from the Scar Girl controversy, this wasn't just about a facial mark; it was a public trial of authenticity. For Gen Z, authenticity is the ultimate currency, and they have honed a sharp instinct to sniff out anything that feels manufactured. To the frustration of many young people, older generations are often less invested in this interactive quest for truth. While they still value authenticity, they also prioritize tradition, stability, and a polished image. For them, respecting rules, regulations, and "the way things have been" is often seen as a virtue.

By contrast, the younger generation feels justified in calling out anything that strikes them as inauthentic. Just as my students took a firm stand on Scar Girl, the younger generation feels compelled to challenge ideas as a way to process information. However, this interrogative style of engagement can be difficult to implement in church settings. If this quest for authenticity uncovers deception, the individual is branded as an "imposter"—a word that has taken on a life of its own in digital culture—to describe a pretender. In a culture that prizes the genuine, this label is devastating, as the person is exposed as a fraud.

Cynicism pervades the cultural landscape. The younger generation has a sharp eye for what they call "performative" behavior—the tendency to present an idealized, "glazed" version of oneself while carefully masking any flaws. To them, this shiny exterior isn't a sign of success; it's a sign of a lack of transparency. Young people today are far too smart to fall for filtered photos and forced happiness. This creates a hurdle for churches that lean into a polished, carefully edited image—a front that often feels more like a performance than a community.

Trained to spot idealized performances, younger generations view staged church programs with skepticism. To them, a polished performance can feel less like an authentic community and more like a strategy designed to win followers. The church risks appearing as though a crafted Christian image matters more than the honest, combative messiness of real engagement. Younger members understand that messiness is a natural by-product of sifting through difficult questions. The struggle is part of the process. Real progress requires walking through real difficulties. When a church sidesteps hard conversations, it signals to a skeptical generation that it is either unable or unwilling to face the truth.

The Gibeonites' Great Deception

The Gibeonites' dirty trick on the Israelites in Joshua 9 highlights a timeless truth: Human have always had a hard time spotting a fake.

When the Gibeonites arrived at the camp gates, the Israelites did their own authenticity policing. They had to determine if these travelers were telling the truth or lying. This historical deception took place while the Israelites were encamped at Gilgal. A group of Gibeonite emissaries arrived, not as themselves, but in a carefully crafted disguise. By posing as weary travelers from a far-off land, they staged an elaborate performance to fake their true intent.

Why the ruse? Against the Israelites, cities and kingdoms fell. Watching from the sidelines, the Gibeonites and their neighbors were filled with dread. The people of Jericho believed they could fend off any invader behind thirteen-foot-tall stone walls and towering twenty-eight-foot watchtowers. They had every reason to feel secure; even before reaching the main gates, attackers had to scale a slick, ten-foot embankment that served as a daunting first line of defense.

Upon arriving at Jericho, Joshua commanded the camp to circle the city, led by priests blowing seven ram's horn trumpets before the Ark of the Covenant. For six consecutive days, they marched around the city as they had been instructed. On the seventh day, they circled the city's perimeter seven times. After the final lap, the blast of the trumpets signaled the Israelites to shout with all their might. Amid the rumblings, "the wall fell down flat" (Joshua 6:20).

The fortifications of Jericho were leveled in extraordinary fashion, sending a deafening boom across the landscape. In the wake of the collapse, Joshua's "fame was in all the land" (Joshua 6:27). The Israelites then turned toward the city-state of Ai, devastating the stronghold and turning it into "a heap of ruins" forever (Joshua 8:28).

With the fall of Jericho and Ai, the Gibeonites knew their turn was coming. It was only a matter of time. They lacked the fortifications and the military infrastructure to withstand such a force. Recognizing that a military confrontation was useless, they hatched a daring scheme with the kind of audacity found in a high-stakes heist movie. A peace treaty was their only option for survival, but the Gibeonites knew the Israelites would never sign one with a local rival that they are were about to conquer, so they cooked up a story about who they were.

Nerves were high as the Gibeonites approached the Israelite camp gates. Clad in their costumes, they signaled to each other and put their fake personas to work. They approached the guards at the entrance. As the guards circled them, the travelers explained they were foreigners who wished to speak with Joshua. The guards saw nothing out of place. The Gibeonites cleared phase one. The guards escorted them to the commander's tent, where a crowd of leaders stared them down, searching every inch of their appearance, from head to toe, for anything dishonest. One wrong word, a nervous twitch, or a visible bead of sweat would have blown their cover and sparked mayhem. But the Gibeonites held their nerve; they didn't blink.

The Gibeonite crew delivered a masterclass in deception the moment they stepped into Joshua's tent. They slumped their shoulders and dragged their feet, ensuring their staged exhaustion was impossible to miss. After brushing off the dust from their disheveled hair and tunics, they explained that they were from a far-off land—yet claimed they had still heard of how the Israelites crushed their enemies. They showered them with praise, recounting how the Israelites had swept through Canaan and toppled every king in their path. They finished making small talk and got serious. The Gibeonite delegation proposed a binding peace treaty—a sacred covenant where both parties would swear to maintain peace. "We have come from a far country," they pleaded, "so now make a treaty with us" (Joshua 9:6).

The Israelites were skeptical. They put the Gibeonite crew under a microscope, looking for the one slip-up that would expose the ruse. The

Israelites weren't buying the story and remained on high alert. "Perhaps you live among us," the Israelites said to them. "How can we make a treaty with you?" (v. 7). Joshua was even more pointed with them, cutting straight to their motives: "Who are you? And where do you come from?" (v. 8).

Their performance was so convincing that it wore down their suspicion. The Gibeonites brushed aside the accusations with a look of disbelief, as if the very idea of deceiving them was absurd. "Your servants have come from a very far country, because of the name of the Lord your God; for we have heard a report of him, of all that he did in Egypt, and of all that he did to the two kings of the Amorites who were beyond the Jordan, King Sihon of Heshbon, and King Og of Bashan who lived in Ashtaroth" (vv. 9–10).

To further sell their fake story, they wore the most tattered rags they could find. The appearance was designed to maintain the illusion that they were foreigners from a distant kingdom, or a people far beyond the Israelites' interests. Having planned the scheme to the last detail, the Gibeonites used stagecraft and accessories to substantiate their story. They laid out their equipment for all to inspect: dusty sacks, ruptured wineskins, and weather-beaten sandals that screamed of a grueling, long-distance journey. They reached into their dusty sacks and pulled out what looked like stones but were old, hard loaves of bread. "Here is our bread; it was still warm when we took it from our houses as our food for the journey, on the day we set out to come to you, but now, see it is dry and moldy" (v. 12).

Providing even more proof, they pointed to the old, cracked wineskins that were strapped to the backs of their tired donkeys. "These wineskins were new when we filled them, and see, they are burst" (v. 13). The Israelites crowded around the pack animals, reaching out to press their fingers into the ruptured gaps of the withered wineskins to physically confirm just how brittle they had become. That was enough proof.

The Israelites were so convinced that they didn't seek "direction from the Lord" (v. 14). Joshua "made peace with them, guaranteeing their lives by a treaty; and the leaders of the congregation swore an oath to them" (v. 15). It wasn't long after they said their goodbyes that the Israelites realized they had been outsmarted. Imagine the shock when, just "three days" later, the Israelites discovered the truth: The foreign emissaries were "their neighbors and were living among them" (v. 16).

Wineskins

The most incredible part of the story, of course, is that the Gibeonites actually pulled it off. It was a gamble that could have easily ended in disaster, but the risk paid off. Between their Oscar-worthy performance and those ruptured wineskins, the Gibeonites successfully stole a peace treaty and saved their people from destruction. Their story was a complete fabrication, yet the worn-out wineskins provided just enough authenticity to convince the Israelites that the lie was worth believing.

For the Israelites, wineskins weren't just liquid containers; they were symbols of their own nomadic roots. Having wandered for forty years in the barren wilderness, a wineskin was an essential tool for survival. Throughout the Israelite camp, leather wineskins of every size hung alongside the tents. Under the relentless desert sun, these skins would eventually harden into stiff, flaky shells—unforgettable symbols of the hardships the people had endured. The perceived shared history was a critical piece of the ruse; because they recognized what they believed to be a common experience, the Israelites immediately sympathized with the Gibeonites' tale.

The Israelites understood better than anyone the labor required to craft a wineskin. To ensure a single, watertight piece, they used traditional slaughtering methods to harvest a whole goat hide. Once cleansed, cured, and tanned, the skin was folded and sewn into a sturdy, kidney-shaped pouch. Living as nomads in the wilderness meant traveling light, making thin leather skins incredibly valuable. When empty, these pouches were surprisingly weightless. They ranged from compact, purse-sized slings for solo travelers to large vessels that required heavy lifting. Because these skins eventually became brittle and prone to rupturing, their production was a constant necessity.

Once sealed inside, the wine is a living, volatile force. As it ferments, it sets off a dynamic sequence of chemical interactions. In short, the grape juice begins its transformation into wine. As the sugar in grapes ferments, it releases carbon dioxide that presses against the goatskin, stretching the leather from the inside out.

The gaseous expansion isn't a problem for a new wineskin; the fresh leather remains flexible enough to stretch under pressure. A new bag has room to grow, making it the only safe choice for new wine. But eventually, that elasticity has its limits, and the skin can no longer expand. While an old wineskin can no longer stretch, its story doesn't end there. These containers are ideal for aged wine—wine that has already finished fermenting and no longer needs to stretch. Jesus uses this dynamic relationship to illustrate a deeper truth in his Parable of the Wineskins (Matthew 9:16–17; Mark 2:21–22; Luke 5:36–39). Jesus said, "No one puts new wine into old wineskins; otherwise the new wine will burst the skins and will be spilled, and the skins will be destroyed" (Luke 5:36–37).

When new wine is poured into new wineskins, they begin a shared journey where both are transformed together. The new wine matures in a safe space, while the new wineskin has the grace to withstand the pressure from the new wine. Such is not the case for old wineskins; they can no longer handle the fermenting power of new wine. It has no more "give." Pairing an old wineskin with new wine creates a destructive relationship; it is the nature of fresh wine to challenge its environment, exerting a steady, expanding pressure that an old vessel simply cannot withstand.

New Wine in Old Wineskins

In the Parable of the Wineskins, think of the established church as a set-in-its-ways vessel—one that has long since lost its ability to stretch. The younger generation represents the volatile energy of new wine, naturally exerting the pressure that demands a new kind of structure. In many churches, the "we've always done it this way" mentality stifles the innovative spirit and leadership potential of the rising generations, preventing their aspirations from ever reaching their full height. We extinguish the spark of creativity that can produce breakthroughs when we force visionary ideas to conform to the way things have always been done.

We must recognize that the rigid, conformist culture we see in churches today was once a vital adaptation to the post-World War II era, when those wineskins were still fresh. In that age, church growth was driven by systematic programs and demographic data—a professionalized approach that relied on experts and ministry specialists to lead the way. Organized, strategic expansion was the primary fermenting agent of that era. But because this focus required specialized studies and professional planning, the average church member often became a passive spectator rather than a participant. Over time, this study-dependent culture caused that wineskin to mature until it finally reached its structural limit.

This expansionist approach worked exceedingly well because the spirit of the time was in alignment with the church's goals. During those decades, the church was a trusted voice for moral clarity and social stability, living in a world where broader cultural values naturally reinforced the reach of religious institutions. Many people in the church are drawn to the old ways because they represent a stability and simplicity that feel absent today. However, the external pillars that once kept the church at the center of community life are not there to hold it up anymore. Social and cultural pillars, such as the high regard for religious institutions, that once protected the church, have crumbled.

The world around the church has shifted, while the church within has stood still. The wineskin from the prosperous postwar era has become today's old wineskin. What happens, then, when this rigid vessel is asked to hold the raw, potent energy of a new generation—the new wine? New wine, by its nature, exerts an internal pressure that the walls of the old wineskin were not meant to withstand. The resulting rupture is often as messy as it is inevitable. While many respond to this tension by rejecting the new wine entirely, we know that option is not sustainable.

In the early 2010s, Eschol United Methodist Church in Wilkesboro was facing permanent closure due to shrinking numbers. In response, the congregation mobilized itself for action—but they did so by leaning into the strategic expansion models of the past that no longer fit the cultural values. In a gesture of radical hospitality, they hosted a free community pasta dinner for all their neighbors. They supported local students by donating stationery and supplies to the elementary school's special needs program. To fight hunger, they organized drives for nonperishable staples, and to refresh their worship, they began renovating the sanctuary from the flooring to the pews. A church member said, "We had made a lot of improvements recently, like putting cushions on the pews and installing new carpet."[41] While the upgrades created a more inviting environment, they failed to generate the response needed to save the church. On June 28, 2015, Eschol gathered for its last Sunday service, closing the doors on a ministry that had first begun in a one-room schoolhouse back in the 1850s.

Strategic expansion isn't just a goal for the old wineskin—it is its defining characteristic. This commitment is deeply woven into the very fabric of the wineskin. The assumption is so powerful that church leaders believe that their survival depends on mastering these strategic models. Even after years of repeated failure, church leaders return to these models, convinced they are the only way to reverse the church's decline and restore it to health.

Take, for example, a large church in a rural town that sprang into action after its attendance was cut in half following the pandemic. Though its finances remained stable, the leaders decided to pour fresh resources into traditional programs, doubling down on outreach and evangelism in a determined attempt to reverse the downward slide. To reach a younger generation, leadership tried to make the outside of the wineskin look different. They introduced a contemporary service, adopting modern styles and tones in an effort to make the old vessel look and feel like something new.

They went "all-in" on children's ministry, launching a wide array of programs designed to serve the needs of young families. Driven by a deep sense of responsibility, they turned their focus outward, increasing their budget to support the "financial needs in the community as much as possible."[42]

Adopting a growth-at-all-costs mentality, the leadership spared no expense on "huge community events" that expanded the church's presence across the region. "Despite its best efforts to grow," the church was surprised at the results: The output of high-quality ministries did little to bring people in. Church attendance stayed the same, still "half of its former size."

CLOSING THOUGHTS

The Parable of the Wineskins is an excellent metaphor for the tensions that exist between a vision for the future and the longing for the past. While most people focus on the disparity between the old and new, many miss Jesus's final observation about why we stay so attached to the past: "No one after drinking old wine desires new wine, but says, 'The old is good'" (Luke 5:39). Simply put, we stick to what we know. The familiar feels safe, while an untested alternative feels like an unnecessary risk.

Change is hard, so we stick with what we've always done—and that is the blind spot Jesus is pointing out. We often mistake the familiar way for the right way. We trust the time-tested path simply because we've walked it so many times, assuming that longevity equals effectiveness. We assume that if a method is institutionally approved, it must be the correct one. We begin to see the established way as superior simply because it is the one we know most intimately. Conversely, if we believe our way is the right way, we assume that anyone doing things differently must be inferior or wrong.

When legacy-bound churches become set in their ways, they transform into old wineskins—rigid vessels unable to stretch or accommodate the pressure of new wine. That is why Jesus says, "New wine must be put into fresh wineskins" (Luke 5:38). But what happens to legacy-bound congregations when they resist letting go of the ways it's always been? An old wineskin will hold up as long as it is filled with old wine—but that supply is disappearing. Legacy-bound congregations will vanish along with it unless they change course and reclaim their flexibility. They must find the courage to venture beyond the boundaries of the comfortable and the familiar, embracing the risks necessary to discover new pathways for the future. Only then will congregations become a place that fuels the imagination of regular people to go beyond what they thought was possible

3

The You-Do-It Challenge

To thrive in today's world, churches are learning to bridge the gap between their heritage and the realities of modern life. They are discovering that while tradition provides the roots, the way they engage with culture must be as fresh and flexible as new wine. This doesn't mean changing the core message, but it does mean realizing that people no longer respond to traditional programs and strategies like they once did. In a digital age where everyone has instant access to worship services and teaching, a local congregation must prove that in-person attendance offers something a podcast cannot. The local church is no longer the only provider of theological information or inspiring messages; it must now provide something deeper.

A critical step in bridging this gap is moving laypeople from the role of quiet observer to that of enkindled innovator. The idea that the regular members should spearhead the church's revival is radical departure from our usual expectations. Within the old vision of strategic expansion, the laity was conditioned to be the recipients of ministry rather than its vanguard. Long-standing church culture reinforces the idea that revitalization is a duty tied strictly to the office of the pastor. *Enkindle* shifts the paradigm.

To propel churches forward, laypeople must stop viewing themselves as unqualified and start seeing themselves as people with the authority to respond to the Holy Spirit's prompting. The people in the pews stay in the background not because they lack talent but because they lack the habit of being self-starters. For churches that truly want to grow, they must be willing to stretch their culture to embrace the movement of the Holy Spirit among the laity. This approach requires a high degree of structural fluidity, where the church body prioritizes the creative input of its members over rigid, outdated growth models. Embracing this mindset means fostering a Spirit-led environment where innovation is discerned and tested, creating pathways to engage the next generation.

The Unexpected Crowd in the "Deserted Place"

At no point in the day did the disciples suspect that a massive gathering would swell around them and a miracle of epic magnitude would then follow. In fact, it was meant to be a quiet day. The day began when messengers arrived to tell Jesus the grim news that John the Baptist, his cousin, had been beheaded by King Herod (Matthew 14:10). Grief-stricken, Jesus told the disciples to find a "deserted place" where he could withdraw in solitude (Matthew 14:13).

They sailed toward a quiet refuge on the northwestern edge of the Sea of Galilee. But as they stepped off the boat, they realized they weren't alone—local villagers were standing by, watching them pull in. Jesus is here! The news raced from village to village in record time. From young children to aging neighbors, people dropped everything in the fields and marketplaces to rush over. This hidden spot was quickly overwhelmed by a crowd larger than anyone could have imagined, as thousands started streaming in "on foot from the towns" (Matthew 14:13).

If he wanted to, Jesus could have simply told the crowd to go home or climbed back into the boat to find a quieter place, yet he chose to stay, for "he had compassion for them" (Matthew 14:14). Pushing in from every side to see Jesus, the crowd kept him from having any downtime to himself. In the meantime, Jesus could be seen spending his time enjoying the company of children and listening to the personal struggles people went through at home; he taught big, complex ideas so simply that even children got it, and would lay hands on those who were suffering and sick.

Gradually, the hours slipped away and the daylight began to fade over the horizon. Realizing the urgency of the situation, the disciples knew they had to act quickly to manage the situation before things got out of hand. They were in a deserted place, far away from any town and much too distant for anyone to reach a village on foot to buy goods. Feeling the tension grow as every minute passed, the disciples looked out at a sea of thousands of people who were looking at them for answers.

After seeing the situation had grown into something they couldn't manage, the disciples knew they had to find Jesus, but it wasn't going to be easy. The disciples pushed through crowds, squeezed in between small gaps, and walked around big groups. When they finally found Jesus, they told him of the situation: "The hour is now late. Send the crowds away so they may go into the villages and buy food for themselves" (Matthew 14:15).

"You Feed Them"

The disciples' request was sensible. They acted out of concern, wanting to ensure that help arrived before it was too late. After the disciples explained the seriousness of the situation, they expected Jesus to give the order to disperse. They were ready to help clear the crowds, but that was not what happened. Jesus would use the moment to challenge their perspective, inviting them to see a bigger reality beyond their human limitations.

After the disciples made their appeal, Jesus paused, letting the weight of the moment sink in. Then, instead of the dismissal they expected, he gave an instruction that left them stumbling for words: "They need not go away; you give them something to eat" (Matthew 14:16). Or, as the New Living Translation puts it even more bluntly: "You feed them."

They were not sure if they heard right. Just thinking about the massive sea of people—"five thousand men, besides women and children" (v.

21)—made their heads spin. The disciples had come to report the trouble; now, the trouble had found them. By pushing them out of their comfort zone, Jesus forced them to face their own limitations. Confused and desperate, they pointed to their meager supply: "We have nothing here but five loaves [of bread] and two fish" (v. 17).

Feeling a bit exasperated, the disciples pointed to their meager supplies to show Jesus just how impossible his request was. They held up the five loaves and two fish as if to say, "This is all we have—and you expect us to feed a city with it?" Desperate and overwhelmed, they cried out, "We have nothing here" (v. 17).

Noticing their defeat, Jesus simply asked them to hand over to him the very thing they called "nothing"—those insignificant loaves and fish they believed were too small to matter. The disciples had no idea a miracle was about to unfold. Jesus then instructed them to tell the scattered thousands to "sit down on the grass," organizing the crowd as if for a grand banquet.

No one could explain what happened next. Jesus "looked up to heaven, and blessed and broke the loaves, and gave them to the disciples" to be distributed to the people" (Matthew 14:19). That "nothing" grew so miraculously that every person in the sea of thousands ate until they were full. After a long day of walking and waiting in the heat, Jesus didn't just meet their needs—he provided such a surplus that the leftovers were piled high.

After everyone had eaten and was completely full, there was still so much food left. The people gathered extra helpings for their long walk home, yet pieces of bread still covered the grass. When the disciples walked around and collected what remained, they filled "twelve baskets full" of bread (v. 20). This specific number—twelve—carries profound symbolic weight, signaling completeness and divine provision, much like the twelve tribes of Israel or the twelve disciples themselves. In Revelation 22:2, the river of life flows through the middle of New Jerusalem, flanked by "the tree of life with its twelve kinds of fruit, producing its fruit each month [of the year that has twelve months]." It remains unclear from the text if the disciples comprehended the significance of the *twelve* baskets left over after the feeding of the five thousand. As each disciple collected a basketful of fragments, it served as a silent, visual correction to their earlier doubt. In the days that followed, they were nourished by the very leftovers they had once dismissed as "nothing."

Pastor Jesus

Imagine Jesus as the pastor of a suburban church. Every Sunday, he explains the meaning of the passage from the pulpit; throughout the week, he provides pastoral care to those going through a hard time and prioritizes visits to the homebound between busy committee meetings. Then, a sudden crisis hits; a heavy snowstorm causes the fellowship hall ceiling to cave in. With the hall shuttered, the congregation is left without a place for coffee hour, community meals, or even youth meeting snacks.

The matter was urgent. They ran to Jesus and explained what had just happened. He listened in silence. Then, as soon as they were done talking, Jesus looked at them and simply said, "You do it." You could imagine them standing there stunned, replaying those words to be sure they had heard him right. Once the shock wore off, they likely found themselves wondering why the pastor wasn't the one taking charge.

Jesus wasn't trying to offload his workload; he was creating a teachable moment. By intentionally stepping back, he created a gap for them to fill—an opportunity to break through. What I call the *you-do-it challenge* is the moment Jesus makes them believe that they can do much more than they ever imagined. It acts as a powerful springboard for innovation, shifting believers away from a passive posture to a dynamic unfolding of their vision. Telling people, "You do it," may seem like a radical, unsettling form of discipleship, but it could well be the key for church members to not only discover the authority they have in Christ but also start using it. This single shift could be the spark that turns the church around.

The Defining Characteristic: Call to Action

The defining characteristic of the you-do-it challenge is its focus on releasing the laity. When Jesus told the disciples, "You feed them," he was speaking to ordinary people who felt completely unqualified for the task. Their first instinct was to send the crowd away. They believed the best way to handle an overwhelming situation was to avoid it or pass the responsibility to someone else.

It is easy for Christians to look at a problem and assume the church or someone else will handle it—much like the disciples did. By telling them, "You feed them," Jesus challenged their learned helplessness by placing them in a situation where they were forced to face their fears and learn to walk in their faith. Jesus also wanted to instill confidence that they were his hands and feet, despite their feelings of inadequacy and lack of preparation.

His command highlights the massive gap between our own self-imposed limits and the boundless potential Jesus sees within us. The disciples looked at the math of the situation and found it didn't add up—five thousand mouths to feed, but only five loaves and two fish. It made no sense. While their logic was technically correct, Jesus wanted them to think beyond the physical. Where they saw a woeful inadequacy, he saw an opportunity. They focused exclusively on what they lacked, forgetting the obvious fact that they were standing right in front of Jesus.

Instead of "You feed them," Jesus could have easily said, "I'll take care of it." He could have resolved the situation singlehandedly, but he stepped back to see if they would finally look beyond their predicament. As a demanding teacher, Jesus was stretching their understanding of what was possible. He didn't just want them to wait for a miracle; he wanted to awaken their own initiative, calling them to move from passive bystanders to active participants in his power.

Throughout the American frontier, church history is rich with accounts of townspeople who—in the absence of clergy—organized their own worship and led the ministries. They decided they could no longer wait for someone else to act. These congregations were the by-product of a grassroots movement started by ordinary local residents without a seminary degree or theological training. While traveling clergy might visit once or twice a month to preach or provide sacraments, it was the local residents who truly owned their religious experience.

Local residents took spiritual matters into their own hands, adopting a you-do-it approach to church. These efforts grew from a deep-seated belief that laypeople were fully capable of leadership. Without official buildings, they gathered wherever they could—fire stations, schoolhouses, town halls, or living rooms serving as makeshift sanctuaries. The work of preaching, leading prayer, and equipping the next generation fell to everyday people who carried no official titles, only a willing spirit.

Instead of waiting for instructions to tell them what to do, these ordinary people took it upon themselves to look after their neighbors, creating a natural bond of trust and accountability. Without a rigid hierarchy, leadership developed organically as people stepped up to meet the needs right in front of them. Because they chose to act without being told, they built a community where people felt like they belonged.

The Second Characteristic: Dream Big

In that isolated, deserted location, the disciples found themselves in a difficult bind: They were surrounded by thousands of hungry people and had no way to feed them. There were no nearby stores or villages to turn to for help. As the crowd grew restless, the disciples ran to Jesus with "nothing." But instead of letting them settle for "nothing," Jesus pushed them to see possibilities far more magnificent than just getting by, which is the second characteristic of the you-do-it challenge.

This characteristic is compelling because it invites us to rewrite the playbook on what is possible. Jesus didn't want the disciples to settle for small goals; he wanted to expand their vision with bold, transformative ideas. He saw that their self-perception was far too narrow, and he pushed them toward a much higher standard of impact. This challenge acts as the spark needed to ignite greatness in anyone—whether they are ten or ninety years old.

We rarely realize how narrow our worldview has become until we are asked to move beyond it. The disciples saw themselves as faithful followers, but Jesus saw them as catalysts for change—capable of the extraordinary with God's help. He understood that transformative power often remains an elusive vision until it is tested by a crisis that exhausts our own ability to manage it. Only by embracing the challenge to act could they move from passive observers to the "I can do all things through Christ" leaders they were meant to be.

Revitalization naturally creates friction between old and new ways. This necessary process is stifled when a church prioritizes a culture of sameness. By upholding conformity as the standard, congregations lose their ability to speak to the complex realities of modern life. They effectively lower the ceiling of what is possible, preventing believers from reaching their fullest expression in Christ.

When Jesus said "You feed them," the command was deeply unsettling—but it was also a radical shift in perspective. By refusing to give a step-by-step breakdown of the task, Jesus signaled that he believed they were capable of more than they imagined. The lack of guidance was, in effect, a tremendous vote of confidence. He was inviting them to bring their own visionary ideas and imaginative energy to the crisis.

The open-ended command gave the disciples a blank canvas, serving as a catalyst for innovation. Jesus was showing them that their participation was more vital than their plan. When laypeople initiate ideas that excite them, they stop being bystanders and start becoming stakeholders in the mission. By encouraging people to pursue their individual passions, a congregation builds deep trust. The fear of failure begins to fade because the community values spiritual growth more than a success-failure paradigm. In this environment, people are free to take calculated risks—which is exactly how the confidence to "walk by faith" is forged.

The Third Characteristic: Be You

A famous actor once shared his philosophy that left the audience stunned: The true art of acting is not to act at all. To most, this sounds counterintuitive. We usually assume an actor's identity is hidden behind a character, like putting on a mask. But he argued that when you are merely pretending to be playing a role, you are showing the world a lie—and the audience can always tell.

He explained that the moment a performer finally stops acting, they shift from pretending to a state of simply being themselves. You bring your true self to the stage, instead of trying to inhabit someone else. While many believe great acting requires maximum effort, that extra strain usually becomes visible and makes the work feel less authentic. Consider what happens when you force a frightened expression through sheer willpower; you don't look scared—you look like a performer struggling to produce a fake emotion.

The audience ends up watching a mechanical effort, but this concept of "not acting" is terrifying for young performers. Why? Because when you decide to strip away the fake layers, it feels like you are standing on stage without any clothes on—completely exposed. To succeed, an actor must be brave enough to drop their guard and stay true to themselves, refusing to cover their flaws. True humility happens when the person on stage focuses on their own performance and starts focusing on the script, the character, and the narrative's emotional truth.

In a similar way, the you-do-it challenge invites us to stop playing a role and start living from our authentic selves. This is the essence of a freestyle approach to growth. In this model, you won't find a road map or growth blueprint; instead, it puts individual passion in the driver's seat. Just as a superb actor's performance feels so natural that you forget they are working, a faith driven by authentic passion avoids the forced, inauthentic feel of someone just going through the motions.

Similarly, freestyle feels natural and effortless. When people see this in action, they see individuals being themselves. Because this authenticity requires no extra effort, it creates an immediate connection with neighbors and seekers. On the other hand, forced expressions create a barrier; people quickly sense an underlying agenda. But when individuals are enkindled in Christ, they aren't operating out of an agenda. They are bringing their true selves to the surface as vessels in the Christ narrative. Just as great actors let the character's breath become their own, freestylers allow the breath of the Holy Spirit to move through their lives.

The Fourth: Self-Discovery in Christ

Taking a step of faith is how you to discover your potential in Christ.

Imagine for a moment if the disciples had actually responded positively to the command, "You feed them." They might have looked at one another in shock before asking the obvious: *How?* But instead of panicking, they could have gathered in a circle and bowed their heads—admitting to God that they were stuck and desperately in need. In that prayer, they would acknowledge that no task is too big for the Lord Almighty, inviting an answer from above.

Let's take how that moment might have unfolded. After acknowledging their limits and anchoring themselves in faith, an idea strikes

Peter. He orders every boat in the area to pull together near the shore. Why? Because he remembers the day on the Lake of Gennesaret when Jesus told him, "Put out into the deep water and let down your nets for a catch" (Luke 5:4). Exhausted and frustrated after a long, fruitless night, Peter didn't want to go back. He had even complained, "Master, we have worked all night long but have caught nothing." Yet, a part of him he couldn't quite explain caused him to pause. "If you say so," he finally replied, "I will let down the nets" (Luke 5:5). With a weary sigh, he called out to his fishing companions to head back out to sea.

They gathered their freshly washed nets and pushed back into the deep. The moment the nets hit the water, Peter felt it—the ropes strained as a massive school of fish swarmed inside all at once. Astonishment quickly turned to fear as the crew struggled to hold the weight. "They caught so many fish that their nets were beginning to break" (v. 6). Peter had never seen anything like it: a silver tide of fish churning beneath the hull.

"They signaled their partners in the other boat to come and help them. And they came and filled both boats, so that they began to sink" (v. 7).

With memories of that overflowing harvest still fresh, Peter calls out to every fishing crew nearby, telling them to gather together immediately. Once they assemble on the shoreline, Peter invites Jesus over to address the crew and boldly asks Jesus to bless them with a new, special harvest. Peter has traded in his wait-and-see attitude; he's found his voice and is being himself by creatively working through the situation in his own freestyle way.

Of course, Peter didn't take this action—but imagine if he had. Picture the impact on the thousands of people witnessing such an event unfold before their eyes. We can almost hear the roar of excitement as the crowd flocks to the shoreline to receive the harvest. Imagine the stories they would tell for generations after seeing such a massive miracle. For the disciples, stepping out in leadership would have reshaped their very souls, fundamentally changing how they viewed themselves and the boundless possibilities of faith.

The fourth characteristic of the you-do-it challenge is a divine spark: the refusal to settle for a predictable narrative in exchange for a thrilling faith adventure. The challenge acts as a launchpad, propelling souls on a quest to discover their truest passions. When an individual's spirit is awakened, it naturally begins to search for a deeper purpose—a truth that resonates with one's unique identity. Finding your authentic self in Christ is more than a personal milestone; it is the spark that ignites innovation within the entire church family.

CLOSING THOUGHTS

Some may wonder if the you-do-it challenge can truly flourish in their church. After all, people often come to find rest and routine, not a new set of challenges. But we shouldn't view this challenge as something that holds us back; it is a key that unlocks the hidden potential of our regular members. When we step beyond the predictable rhythms of religious life, we get a glimpse of something higher. This realization doesn't drain us—it breaks the monotony, offering a powerful new perspective on what it means to truly live in Christ.

Just as Jesus stirred the waters when he told his disciples, "You feed them," the you-do-it challenge will upset the calm. It also introduces a divine interruption that forces us to reimagine what we are capable of. Responding to this call produces a spark of energy that makes us feel alive in Christ, moving us from the sidelines to become active participants in God's unfolding plan.

Jesus commanded his disciples to feed the masses knowing full well that the task would leave them feeling confused and overwhelmed. This was intentional; the challenge was designed to reveal the limits of our own abilities. Until that moment, the disciples had been spectators of the miraculous, bearing witness to awe-inspiring moments. Now, Jesus was calling them to move from watching his power to carrying it out themselves. He was pushing them to "walk by faith" and "not by sight" (2 Corinthians 5:7).

The you-do-it challenge fundamentally changes how a church views its people. If we want our congregations to thrive, we have to realize that our great resource isn't our buildings, our history, or our strategic visions—it is the everyday people sitting in the pews. For a congregation to be effective in the twenty-first century, it nurtures people whose hearts are on fire with purpose and then releases their passion outward. Only when a congregation's guiding ethos shifts from preservation to empowerment will the church truly thrive in the decades to come.

4

Rethinking Lay Engagement

In Acts 4:13, the Sanhedrin questioned Peter and John and labeled them *idiotes* (ἰδιώτης), the Greek term from which we get "idiot," but it's not what you think. Rather than an insult, the word expressed the Sanhedrin's astonishment at the disciples' impressive speaking skills despite their common backgrounds. In this context, *idiotes* refers to a "private person," "layman," or "unskilled"—someone without formal professional status. While translations like the NRSV and NIV use "ordinary" or "untrained," the term never implies a lack of actual skill or worth; it simply meant they weren't part of the official system.

In the ancient world, an *idiotes* was simply someone unengaged in political affairs or lacking formal training in religious texts. It served as a contrast between the everyday person and those of rank—whether a magistrate, a trained orator, or, within Jewish circles, a trained rabbi. While the word sounds harsh to modern ears, it was standard vocabulary at the time. It was a common way to differentiate social backgrounds, and Peter and John likely would have accepted the description without offense or argument.

Jesus found them along the Sea of Galilee, simply going about their day. Peter and Andrew were casting nets into the surf (Mark 1:16–17), while John and James were with their father, Zebedee, mending theirs (Mark 1:19–20). Both pairs had been raised in the fishing industry, their education a hands-on apprenticeship that began as soon as they were old enough to help. They knew every detail of their subculture: from the grunt work of scrubbing massive nets to the skill of steering through fierce waves; from the art of reading weather patterns to the instinct for tracking fish; and finally, the business acumen required to negotiate their catch at the market.

Peter and John weren't born into privileged circles; they lived simple, no-nonsense lives of everyday people. What kept them grounded was a deep connection to the typical struggles of survival—problems that were woven into their daily experience. While religious scholars debated the finer points of the Law, these men were locked into the real world. They headed out to work early every morning, just like anyone on today's commute. For them, a connection to God was formed through the lens of a daily routine. Whether repairing a car engine, assisting a patient, stocking grocery shelves, or waiting tables, our own work serves as that same bridge—connecting our lived experience to our understanding of faith.

Peter and John were regular guys whose lives were set ablaze by a life-changing encounter with Jesus. In this chapter, we will look at other ordinary individuals—people without titles or theological degrees—who felt a deep pull from God to serve their communities. People like Casey Diaz, Lucy Blaylock, MC Jin, and Dorothea Dix prove that you already have everything you need to be fruitful. We often wrongly assume only ministry professionals can grow a congregation, but ordinary people receive distinct leadings from God too. They don't start with a strategic plan; they simply follow God's voice. Because they lack a formal ministerial outlook, they can connect authentically with other regular people, especially with their subculture. We can transform our congregations the moment we unlock this untapped missional force hidden in our pews.

Casey Diaz

"Let your light shine before others."
Matthew 5:16

Casey Diaz was a notorious violent offender.

Before he even stepped foot inside New Folsom State—a maximum-security facility near

Sacramento, California—the inmates and prison staff already knew his name. On his first day, a guard led him to a private room, holding a folder that had his name on the front. "Listen closely, Diaz," the guard said. "We know that you're a banger and a shot caller, so we're putting you in solitary."[43] Instead of adding him to the inmate population, they locked Diaz away in solitary confinement because he was a "shot caller," a high-ranking gang leader who gave the orders to commit murders and decided, in effect, who lives and who doesn't. He was sixteen years old when he entered New Folsom State with a sentence of over twelve years. The legal system came down hard, convicting him of a second-degree murder charge and fifty-two counts of armed robbery.

As a boy, Diaz's life felt more like a battlefield than a childhood, marred by poverty and abuse. At just eleven years old, he fled his home to join the Rockwood Street Locos, a gang that became his surrogate family. He climbed the ranks fast, surpassing older members through a ruthless commitment to violence. "I led the way," Diaz recalled, "when we invaded homes, broke into cars, ransacked convenience stores, and stabbed rival gang members."[44] His brutal efficiency was so absolute that, despite his youth, he was promoted to the rank of "shot caller."

It didn't take long for the law to catch up with him. At New Folsom, solitary confinement meant an eight-by-ten-foot windowless cell, severed from the rest of the world. Day after day, the oppressive silence was broken only by the scrape of a food tray sliding through a thin slot in the steel door. Locked in that cramped void, Diaz began to wonder if he actually had the strength to endure it.

After a year, Diaz was lying on his bunk when he heard voices outside his door. A woman with a slow, Southern drawl pointed to a cell and asked the guard, "Is there someone in that cell?" The guard didn't hesitate, "Yes, ma'am, but you don't want to deal with Diaz. You're wasting your time." Listening from the other side, Diaz silently agreed with the guard's assessment. He had been an unrepentant gangbanger since he was eleven years old—but this woman wasn't deterred."

"Well," she told the guard, "Jesus came for him, too."[45]

She got closer and asked, "Young man, can I speak with you?"

Diaz approached the steel door and peered through the open slot.

"I couldn't see anything except for the guard's boots and a pair of spindly legs," Diaz recalled.

"How are you doing?" she asked.

"Couldn't be better," he replied.

Unfazed, she said, "Young man, I'm going to pray for you. but there's something else I want to tell you: Jesus is going to use you."

The suggestion felt like a bizarre joke. To a man set to remain in a windowless void for the next decade, her words made no sense. The idea that he could be useful for anything, let alone for God, felt like nonsense.

"Don't think that's going to happen," he replied.

"Young man, every time I'm here, I'm going to come by and remind you that Jesus is going to use you," she persisted.

One day, while lying on his bunk, Diaz saw a vision. Vivid scenes began playing across his cell wall like a movie—except he was the main character, and he knew the tragic ending of every scene. He saw himself as a young boy in his old neighborhood, making reckless choices in "picture-perfect detail." As the images flickered against the cold stone, the weight of his past finally broke through his armor, filling him with a profound, unshakable sadness.

The movie then shifted to a man Diaz had never met. He was bearded, with long hair, struggling under the crushing weight of a wooden cross he was carrying. Diaz watched as the man endured agonizing physical pain while a hostile crowd screamed insults and hate. The scene continued: The man staggered to the top of a hill and was forced onto the beams he had been carrying. Iron nails were driven through his hands and feet, fastening him to the wood. As the soldiers hoisted the cross upright, the man let out a guttural groan of agony that echoed through the small cell.

The movie then zoomed in, focusing entirely on the face of the man hanging on the cross. Slowly, he turned his head until his gaze locked onto Diaz. In that moment, their eyes met.

"Darwin, I'm doing this for you," the man said.

He was stunned to hear the man speak his real name: Darwin. He had gone by Casey for years; only his family and prison guards knew his birth name. Before he could even process how this stranger knew him, he watched him struggle for one last, shallow breath—and die.

Startled by what had just happened, he "hit the floor in the middle of the cell."

"I started weeping because I knew, somehow, that this was Almighty God, even though I didn't understand what he had done for me. After hitting the floor, I knew I had to get on my knees."

In that moment, he started confessing his sins: "God, I'm sorry for stabbing so many people; I'm sorry I robbed so many families."

Instinctively, he fell to his knees, confessing and asking forgiveness for every act of violence and every bad decision he had ever made. He described the moment as if a massive "weight come off my shoulders."

His heart was set ablaze.

"I knew something major had happened."

Diaz immediately asked to see a chaplain and recounted the vision exactly as it had played out on his cell wall. As he spoke, the chaplain began to tremble, tears welling in his eyes. Diaz recalled, "His bottom lip started to shake and he opened the Bible. He started to read about the crucifixion and Him [Jesus] walking to Golgotha [the place where Jesus died]. When he started to read that we both broke. A lot of tears were shed in that moment because I knew that's what I had seen. No one had ever told me that."[46]

He felt a burning desire to know everything about the bearded man who had spoken his name. With the Bible that the chaplain gave him, Diaz began to devour the Bible. "If I was awake," he recalled, "I would read it and read it and read it." He spent every waking hour in that cell either lost in Scripture or deep in prayer. Then, one day, the heavy silence of solitary was broken when God spoke: "When you get out of here, you are going to gather your homeboys, your gang leaders and you're going to let them know you want nothing to do with this anymore, that you are now a Christian."[47]

Diaz was ready, but he was in solitary confinement, and wondered how this would happen. Then, in a stunning turn of events, he was moved back to the general population. "To this day I don't know why," he said. "I know it was ordained by God." As he stepped onto the prison yard, his gang members rushed to greet him, but they stopped short—they could see something had changed. Taking a deep breath, Diaz gathered them and described how Jesus had met him in that cell. As he spoke, their faces were a mirror of the angry, lost man he had been only months before. Looking into their empty eyes, he saw the destruction waiting for them. He begged them to reconsider their ways, to walk away, and to discover the true freedom in Christ.

Needless to say, they didn't take it well. They stood in stunned disbelief, unable to process the fact that their shot caller was now preaching to them about Jesus. For them, this was an intolerable betrayal. They didn't just walk away; they turned their backs on him—a silent, chilling signal in gang code that he was a dead man walking. Diaz knew the rules. He knew exactly what that silence meant: A hit was coming.

The next morning, Diaz sat on the edge of his bunk, gripping his Bible. He accepted it; he was simply waiting for the moment they would show up. Sure enough, a gang member stepped into the cell clutching a prison-made shank. But as the man looked at Diaz, he found he couldn't strike. Diaz's testimony in the yard touched his heart so much that he became a believer, becoming the very first person that Diaz led to Christ.

No matter how many times they threatened his life, Diaz refused to retreat. He had turned his back on his past, and was determined never to return. He was beaten severely and often, but he decided he would rather take a brutal beating than participate in the gang's violence. He ended up in the infirmary so many times that he eventually lost count of the treatments, the stitches, and the scars. For Diaz, every bruise was proof of a faith that was no longer a performance—it was his life.

By the time Diaz walked out of the gates of New Folsom State, the boy who had entered was gone. He emerged with a new mission: to testify of his Savior to inmates, gang members, and anyone else who would listen. As he famously put it, "I was no longer a shot caller. I had found a new calling." In his book, *The Shot Caller*, Diaz recounts that journey from the violent streets of Los Angeles to the encounter with Jesus in solitary confinement.[48] Today, he uses his platform at conferences and retreats to broadcast the same radical love and redemption that rescued him.[49]

Lucy Blaylock

"Let the little children come to me; do not stop them; for it is to such as these that the kingdom of God belongs."
Mark 10:14

While Casey Diaz experienced a sudden, dramatic revelation, most believers find their purpose through a much quieter process. Rather than a single lightning-bolt moment, many discover their calling incrementally, with clarity surfacing over time. God often leads us step by step toward a deeper realization of who we are in Christ. For instance, when eight-year-old Lucy Blaylock hand-stitched her first blanket for a friend's birthday, she had no idea that this simple act of kindness was the seed of a global nonprofit.

Watching her friend adore that handmade gift lit a fire in Lucy's heart. For the first time, she felt the thrill of making a tangible impact through a simple act of kindness. Encouraged, she decided to sew more—but this time, for a cause. She wanted to comfort children facing their own heavy struggles. She and her mother posted a simple message on Instagram: They were looking for nominations for any child who needed a blanket. The only requirement? That the child needs love. They posted it and waited, having no idea if anyone would actually respond.

In a single day, sixteen heartfelt nominations arrived. As she read stories of children enduring the pain of divorce, the grief of loss, or the ordeal of severe illness, a curtain was pulled back on the world. Lucy was no longer just a girl with a hobby; she was witnessing a reality she could not ignore. This revelation fundamentally changed her perspective, proving that you don't need to be an adult to have your heart broken by what breaks God's. Lucy recalled: "I just could not stand the thought of any of these kids going without a blanket. So I made one for all 16 of those children and shipped it to them [free of charge]."[50]

As word spread, the requests began to pour in. Lucy stayed true to her founding principle: If a child needed love, they were eligible. Soon, stories were arriving from all corners of the country. Confronted with a growing mountain of need, Lucy didn't overthink the strategy or wait for a master plan. As she simply put it, "So I started sewing, and kept sewing because I kept getting requests." Each blanket is hand-stitched by Lucy herself and mailed out at no cost, ensuring that every child selected receives a tangible gift of love.

Every blanket is a labor of love. As Lucy spends two or three hours hand-sewing for an individual, she keeps that child's story in the front of her mind. She mentions them by name, lifting their specific struggles up in prayer. As Lucy explains, "What is really cool is that I know the story of that child while I'm making his or her blanket, which means I can pray for the child the whole time I'm making it."

By the time 2023 came to a close, Lucy managed to sew more than 1,100 blankets since she first started the project that came to be known as "love blankets." They have reached every state and seventeen foreign countries so far. She sews a small heart by hand on every blanket so the child who gets it will always remember that someone loves them. You might wonder why she cares so much about kids. It all goes back to what Jesus taught her. "If Jesus were still on earth," Lucy believes he would be "making these kids feel loved and supported." When she looks at her life and her future, Lucy believes that nothing matters more than being a blessing to others. She sees this not just as a hobby, but as her specific role in God's larger plan. As Lucy explains, "I'm just trying to be His hands here on earth by making these blankets. I think kindness always matters, and always will. It makes the world a better place when we do kind acts for one another."

Lucy never imagined her small act of kindness would grow into a global nonprofit. Today, thanks to generous donors, she ships love blankets to children around the world.[51] She may lack formal ministry titles or theological training, but her passion has proven to be more than enough to change lives. For a child enduring the darkest of hardships, they can now literally wrap themselves in the love and prayers Lucy stitched into every fiber of their blanket.

Our culture is not only transactional but deeply disconnected. We often approach relationships by asking, "What am I getting out of this?" viewing people as resources or stepping stones rather than neighbors. Sadly, this mindset often bleeds into the church. We go "church shopping" for the perfect program or style, while volunteering feels like just another item on a to-do list. When a church thinks of members as consumers, it naturally obsesses over performance: the lighting, the production, and the amenities. It becomes a business to be managed rather than a family to belong to.

The beauty of Lucy's love blankets lies in their absolute lack of an agenda. She asks for nothing in return—not even a thank-you note. In a transactional world, her blankets stand out as a rare example of love with no strings attached. Because of this transparency, they carry a weight of authenticity that is difficult to find. Even those prone to cynicism would struggle to find fault here; Lucy isn't trying to advance an interest or build a brand. She is simply being herself.

Churches can come across as having an agenda. If you don't fit a certain mold or follow their specific set of rules, support can feel conditional. However, when congregations enable their church members to release their deepest passions, they not only encourage their people to boldly walk in faith but also build a network of authentic relationships in their community. People like Lucy show us that young people in particular can transform their local church communities. Local congregations have the opportunity to create a space where their young people can stretch, explore, and discover their own voices and learn to communicate their own stories about what Jesus means to them.

MC Jin

"Now the Lord is the Spirit; and where the Spirit of the Lord is, there is freedom."
2 Corinthians 3:17

Better known as MC Jin, Jin Au-Yeung drops a line in one of his tracks where he asks a question, "Guess what?" before happily revealing the news that "I'm brand new."[52] He opens up about the big changes in his personal life, showing everyone he's a different person than he used to be. "Even if you don't know me, all you need to know is that I ain't the old me and tomorrow is a brand new day. As long as I got God, everything's OK."

Au-Yeung's transformation is fascinating. After starting out as a rapper and actor, he shifted his focus and his music to the Lord. For the fans who had followed him since his early days, the release of the *Brand New Me* EP was quite a surprise—a bold announcement that he was now following Jesus. Before this turning point, Au-Yeung had built a reputation as a gritty, street-savvy lyricist, a talent he had been honing since he was a teenager. He was only nineteen when he became a breakout star by defeating seven straight opponents in rap battles on BET's television program "106 & Park." His amazing streak of wins on the broadcast led to his induction into the show's Hall of Fame. The music world took notice. He secured a high-profile recording contract, making him the first Chinese American solo rap artist to sign with a major label.

As his music career gained traction, Au-Yeung's influence spread beyond hip-hop. His story was featured in national outlets like *Time* magazine, and he soon transitioned into Hollywood. He made his acting debut in the 2 *Fast* 2 *Furious* franchise, playing Jimmy, a mechanic known for his expertise under the hood. For a time, it seemed he had reached his ultimate goal: living the wealthy, famous lifestyle he had always dreamed of. "I just signed a record deal, pretty much had all the things I had dreamed and desired for ever since the age of 16," he remarked. "At the age of like 16, 17 during my high school years, I had the most conscious and dedicated and committed mindset in terms of these are the things that I'm pursuing: a rap career, stardom, fame, money, finances, girls, houses, cars."[53]

As the years passed, more roles in big-budget films helped Au-Yeung gain fans worldwide. On the surface, it appeared he had finally "made it," and he was now able to buy everything on his wish list. Behind the scenes, however, his life was crumbling. He began to lose his sense of identity, and when his career stalled and the phone stopped ringing, he slid toward a sense of total meaninglessness. As he put it: "As quick as that [success] happened is as quick as I kind of vanished into obscurity."[54] Sinking into a deep depression, he withdrew from the world, spending his days alone and silent.

While lost in a very dark place, Au-Yeung rediscovered the faith of his childhood. His return to God wasn't a loud or sudden event, but a quiet stirring deep in his soul that prodded him to rethink his life. He began to look at his past and wonder if he had been chasing the wrong things; the more he pursued fame and luxury, the more hollow he felt inside. Eventually, he embraced a humbling truth: God meant more than everything else. "The acting, the TV dramas, and everything else were all great experiences," he said, "but it does not compare at all to the experience of God's presence in my life."[55] The fact that God never gave up on him, even at his worst, captured Au-Yeung's heart. "What's really stood out to me," he reflected, "is what God has been showing me in terms of understanding what His love and grace truly mean."

On the track "Hallelujah" from the *Brand New Me* album, Au-Yeung bared his soul about how close he came to giving up. "I thought it was comin' to a end [sic]," he raps. "My career was comin' to a end, my journey was comin' to a end." At this personal low, he credits a divine intervention for his recovery: "God, you picked me up and You lifted me up and showed me that what I thought was the end was really just the beginnin.'" This song serves as his ultimate declaration of a life turned around: "So all I ask Lord is that, From here on out, That You be the center."

Au-Yeung's music was once defined by the combative "gangsta rap" persona of the hip-hop world, a sound that has softened since his spiritual breakthrough. While the church often dismisses hip-hop dialect as "profane" or unfit for sacred expression, a significant portion of the younger generation views the world through that very lens. By refusing to engage with hip-hop culture, the church risks losing its ability to connect with a generation's language and perspective. Although Au-Yeung's life has changed, his medium remains hip-hop. He engages young people in a way traditional outreach often misses; by speaking with the linguistic nuances of the streets, he builds authentic Christian bridges to a generation that frequently feels misunderstood by traditional institutions.

Because laypeople excel within their own subcultures, they possess a vernacular that feels natural, whereas the church's attempts to imitate them can feel like a condescending effort to be relevant. Au-Yeung is a native speaker of his subculture; he translates profound truths to the "street level" of his peers without losing the message's impact. Because individuals like him carry inherent credibility within their niche communities, they don't need a formal program or method to reach people—they just have to be themselves. Au-Yeung is still MC Jin, but he is now on a different mission. As he puts it: "As long as the music is being heard by whoever God wants and that He is receiving the glory, nothing else matters."[56]

Dorothea Dix

"If we live by the Spirit, let us also be guided by the Spirit."
Galatians 5:25

Dorothea Dix (1802–1887) never imagined spearheading a national movement. However, after her first visit to the East Cambridge House of Correction on March 28, 1841, she was enkindled with compassion for those struggling with mental disorders—and a righteous anger against the system that failed them. Dix had gone to East Cambridge simply to teach a Sunday school class to women inmates; instead, she was horrified to find the mentally ill incarcerated in inhumane conditions alongside hardened criminals. Witnessing such cruelty only strengthened her resolve to take action.

In a petition to the Massachusetts legislature, Dix chronicled the appalling conditions she had witnessed. She described men, women, and children—half-naked and underfed—chained to walls in what she called "dungeon cells." "I have come to present to you the strong claims of suffering humanity," Dix wrote. "I come as the advocate of the helpless, forgotten, insane men and women held in cages, closets, cellars, stalls, pens! Chained, naked, beaten with rods, and lashed into obedience!"[57] She described a woman inmate "in the horrid process of tearing off her skin by inches; her face, neck, and person, were thus disfigured to hideousness."

Dix found these same conditions everywhere she went—whether in jails, poorhouses, or houses of correction. Having traveled the state to survey its facilities, she reported that the mentally ill were often kept in filthy sheds that lacked sunlight, heat, and ventilation. In one location after another, they were abandoned in wet, foul-smelling outbuildings and left to rot in dark corners. This systematic neglect stripped them of their dignity and their very sense of humanity. In her detailed accounts, Dix described men and women who had been chained to walls for so long they had regressed into primitive desperation, resembling wild animals more than people.

Although the harsh treatment of the era was often accepted as normal, Dix refused to remain silent. Her dogged campaigning earned her the moniker "Voice for the Mad," and her activism compelled Massachusetts to fund its first dedicated treatment center. Building on this success, Dix traveled over thirty thousand miles across the country, uncovering similar horrors in every state she visited. She spent the next several years petitioning legislatures nationwide, tirelessly fighting to replace "dungeon cells" with proper, humane institutions for the downtrodden and forgotten.

For Dix, this was never merely a job; it was a "sacred cause." As a woman of deep faith, she viewed her reform work as a "manifestation of the Lord's will."[58] When she began her mission in 1843, there were only thirteen mental institutions in the entire country—a reflection of a society that viewed the mentally ill as criminals or outcasts. By reframing the care of the vulnerable as a moral and religious responsibility, she helped that number grow to 123 institutions, playing a direct role in the founding of 32 of them.

In the beginning, Dorothea Dix was simply a schoolteacher looking for a quiet way to serve. She never intended to become the firebrand and reformer we remember today. She possessed no strategic plan, no background in the prison system, and no degree in law or public policy. Yet, this ordinary woman single-handedly changed how we treat the mentally ill after her heart was set ablaze by the cruelty she witnessed. Dix was an outsider, but her story serves as a reminder that regular people—including church members today—should never feel that a lack of credentials limits their impact. She is a powerful example that expertise is not a prerequisite for change; rather, it is the fire of passion and a commitment to follow through on one's principles that truly transforms society.

CLOSING THOUGHTS

"Do not quench the Spirit."
1 Thessalonians 5:19

Four individuals of different eras and backgrounds—Casey Diaz, Lucy Blaylock, Jin Au-Yeung, and Dorothea Dix—each felt a profound pull toward action after a spark was lit within them. They reached a point where they could no longer sit still; it was as if a light had been switched on. This is the "enkindled" moment—when an ordinary person is ignited by the Holy Spirit and filled with the drive to serve a subculture, a specific demographic, or a marginalized community.

Casey Diaz grew up in a world where violence was the primary currency of survival. On these contested battlegrounds, he knew that danger followed him everywhere; you couldn't walk down the street without looking over your shoulder, wondering if a rival was waiting around the corner to pounce. As an insider, Diaz understands the claustrophobic mindset of those trapped in the gang cycle. When he preaches on themes of personal redemption and liberation in Christ, he knows these concepts ring differently to those on the streets—hitting them with the force of a powerful internal explosion.

Lucy Blaylock was not even ten years old when she started making her love blankets. She serves as a reminder that children are capable of starting global movements; while we often view children as recipients of care, they can also be innovators of pastoral work. From a modest sewing table, Lucy has extended her ministry across borders and inspired an ever-increasing number of donors to support her global nonprofit. Imagine if congregations helped unleash that kind of passion among children within their own communities. When a church nurtures a small seed, they may be surprised to see how the faith of a child can blossom in ways they never imagined.

While many in the church are unfamiliar with hip-hop, a vast portion of today's youth culture is shaped by its trends, style, and sound. When MC

Jin raps about the gospel, he isn't an outsider mimicking the culture; he is a native of it. By using the familiar slang, rhythms, and metaphors of the street, he translates the gospel into a language the hip-hop generation can truly respect. He proves that the message of Jesus can be expressed through contemporary, rhythmic storytelling, creating a journey of redemption that his listeners find deeply relatable.

Within the pews of our local congregations lies a hidden resource: ordinary people whose lives outside the sanctuary provide them with profound, insider knowledge of subcultures and the neighborhoods the church seeks to reach. These individuals are often the first to sense the shifting needs and aspirations of the community—long before those trends appear on a ministry's radar. Because they possess a level of trust and legitimacy that traditional programming cannot reproduce, their unique cultural insights are invaluable. When congregations become facilitators of these unique gifts, they aren't just filling roles; they are investing in the next generation of innovators.

5

Releasing Enkindled Souls

An overlooked hero in Casey Diaz's story is Frances Proctor, who sought out the hardened gang leader while he was in solitary confinement. She braved a prison environment to reach a man most of society would have preferred to leave for dead. Even when guards warned her, "Don't waste your time," she felt a divine nudge toward him—an act of obedience that would spark a miraculous transformation. When she first approached his cell, however, Diaz felt only dread. "I wanted nothing to do with her or her religion," he recalled. "I never went to church. I had no biblical knowledge, didn't care about God, wasn't looking for God."[59]

"Well, I'm going to put you on my prayer hit list and Jesus is going to use you," she replied.

"This lady is nuts," thought Diaz. "She has no clue about what she's doing here or who she's talking to."[60] Diaz was probably right. She didn't know his rap sheet or his connections to a violent gang, but it didn't matter to Proctor whether Diaz was a petty thief or a high-ranking gang leader. Her mission was defined by her faith rather than his sentencing.

The commitment shown by Frances Proctor illustrates how a spirit set ablaze by conviction remains internally driven, regardless of unfavorable surroundings. For ordinary church members whose hearts have been ignited, this higher purpose becomes a self-sustaining drive that requires no external prompting. The weight of their convictions creates a natural forward momentum that persists no matter the challenges before them.

This chapter takes a closer look at five ordinary individuals—a retiree, a child, a cafeteria employee, and two teenagers—to help us understand the wide-ranging passions people carry, regardless of age. Everyone, without exception, possesses a pursuit that defines their sense of purpose. When someone cares deeply about a cause, they tap into a hidden reservoir of strength that enables them to love what they do and persevere through any challenge. Far more than a mere hobby, an individual's passion is a flame of excitement—a powerful force that can reshape a person's entire life.

Now, imagine that human flame enkindled by the fire of the Holy Spirit. The result is a spiritual combustion—a powerful force that reshapes a person's identity. When an individual lives from this enkindled core, their motivation becomes part of their faith DNA, a self-sustaining drive that no longer craves worldly validation. This spirit is internally generated and divinely fueled. Therefore, a vital mission of the local congregation is to identify and nurture these raw passions, helping individuals unleash their unique callings to serve the community and the world.

To empower spirit-led individuals, local congregations must navigate between the impulse to reinforce institutional identity and encouraging individual calling. The possibility of ordinary people expressing Jesus as a natural overflow of their lives is the core of the *Enkindle* vision—and it may well be the breakthrough the church has been waiting for. However, this breakthrough is impossible if churches resist the boundary-pushing initiatives of their members. By de-emphasizing conformity and embracing radical trust, congregations unlock a latent energy capable of reaching communities once thought unreachable. Fostering this self-motivated faith allows the church to evolve into a diverse religious ecosystem rather than a rigid, monocultural organization.

A Solution to Overwhelmed Clergy

In the opening chapter, we explored the growing crisis of pastoral burnout and the exodus of leaders from the ministry. Many enter the field with a desire to participate in God's plan, only to find that plan buried under a mounting backlog of administrative tasks. The sheer volume of a pastor's responsibilities is often invisible to the average churchgoer. While we see them behind the pulpit or offering care at community events, the behind-the-scenes reality is a relentless cycle of managing budgets, leading staff, overseeing facility maintenance, and remaining on standby for 24/7 emergencies. Mark Batterson, lead pastor of National Community Church in Washington, DC, aptly describes this overwhelming reality:

I think a pastor used to be viewed as the one-stop ministry shop. The pastor served on every committee, volunteered at every event, and made all the hospital visits. I think that is changing and I think that is healthy. Both for the pastor and the congregation. In a sense, I think we've cultivated a codependency in our churches. We expect the pastor to pray for us, study for us, disciple our kids for us.[61]

Beyond these administrative burdens, the pastor is also expected to be the primary engine of church growth. The congregation often views the pastor as the chief growth officer, solely responsible for increasing attendance and the membership roll. This pressure intensifies when numbers dip; the pews turn toward the pulpit, expecting the pastor to make things happen and draw people back into the sanctuary. Consequently, the pastor becomes the architect of every detail—from ensuring there are greeters at the door and coffee in the lobby to designing the perfect path for newcomers to get connected.

Often, the pastor is expected to be the visionary—the one tasked with coming up with creative projects to attract those outside the church walls. But consider a different paradigm: What if the pastor no longer carried the burden of church growth alone? What if the responsibility for expansion shifted to the congregation itself? Such a transition would do more than just lift a heavy weight off the pastor's shoulders; it would transform the very nature of how the church grows.

Consider the manifold possibilities when a church truly unleashes its people to live out their faith. Imagine a congregation where laypeople create and innovate through a shared mission—where the pews become a collective think tank, enabling members to commit their unique backgrounds to a unified vision. In this paradigm, growth happens naturally. When members take responsibility for expansion, their sense of ownership deepens; they are no longer just attendees, but active architects of the church's future. Perhaps most importantly, this model creates long-term sustainability. If a pastor leaves or retires, the congregation doesn't lose momentum, because the motivation and movement come from the people themselves.

Frances Proctor

Driven by a spiritual calling, Frances Proctor led a small prayer team from South Central Los Angeles to visit inmates at New Folsom State in Sacramento—a daunting six-hour journey. She wasn't merely filling a church volunteer position; "Mother Proctor," as she was affectionately known by her African American church, was motivated by a deep compassion to bring light to those languishing in solitary confinement.

Mother Proctor understood that even a small act of kindness can shift a person's trajectory. While inmates often maintain a mean and crusty exterior, Casey Diaz speaks from experience when he says, "A little compassion can go a long way. A quick visit, a few prayers, or a card in the mail could be the difference that helps them make it through."[62] Although the guards allowed Mother Proctor only a few minutes at his cell door, those brief moments changed everything. As Diaz recalled, they "made all the difference in me believing I could have a new life."

Initially, her talk of Jesus drew only sneers of disbelief from Diaz. But Mother Proctor was persistent. "Well," she told him, "I'm going to put you on my prayer hit list, and Jesus is going to use you."[63] She was true to her word. For the next eighteen months, she made the long trek to New Folsom State once a month just to intercede for him. Every time she stood before his cell in solitary confinement, she repeated that same phrase: "Jesus is going to use you." Slowly, those seeds began to take root. As Diaz later admitted, "It began to make me wonder."[64]

Mother Proctor's passion was reaching those whom society had forgotten and abandoned. She followed a deep-seated conviction that, through Christ, no one is beyond hope. While others saw Casey Diaz as a lost cause—just another failure who got what he deserved—Mother Proctor saw him through the eyes of faith. To her, he was a redeemable child of God, regardless of his past.

Just as Diaz thought she was crazy, many in her own church likely felt the same. How many transformative ideas have local congregations rejected simply because they sounded too "out there" or unconventional? Mother Proctor refused to give up on a "lost cause," and we must do the same for our own members. When they come to us with big, unusual visions, we need to offer belief instead of skepticism.

Mother Proctor was certain that Jesus would use Diaz, but she likely never imagined how that promise would unfold. Because an enkindled fire can move in any direction, congregations must be elastic enough to stretch and allow that self-motivated energy to lead the way. Imagine her surprise when she learned that Casey Diaz had helped lead two hundred inmates to Christ within the walls of New Folsom. Beyond witnessing in the yard and the chow hall, Diaz sent "kites"—handwritten notes passed between cells. While others used kites to relay gang orders, Diaz used them to send love notes from God. "One of the founding members of [the notorious] MS-13 came to Christ through one of those kites," Diaz recalled, "then another gang leader from South Central."[65] The church's greatest era of expansion will be defined by its ability to discern, encourage, and let the light of such enkindled souls shine.

Joshua Whitehouse and LEGO Ministry

Joshua Whitehouse built a global ministry one brick at a time—literally. However, in the beginning, he had no intention of creating a ministry; it happened by accident. A self-described "LEGO nerd," Whitehouse was hooked the moment he received his first set at five years old. While LEGO sets come in a vast array of themes and licensed universes, they weren't enough for him. The creative challenge of the bricks ignited his imagination. As Whitehouse recalls, "Very quickly, I began taking them apart and creating my own builds."[66]

Seeing how he innovated new designs from various sets, Joshua's mother suggested he use his talent to illustrate Bible stories. The idea took shape during the COVID-19 lockdowns, a time when families were stuck at home and unable to attend church. She approached him with a simple request: "Hey, can you make a Bible story out of LEGO for the Sunday School class?" Whitehouse, then a teenager and already an accomplished builder, thought, "That's a cool idea, why not give it a try?" Having already competed in online LEGO challenges, creating a stop-motion Bible story felt like a natural next step—or, as he put it, "very simple."

Throughout the lockdown, Whitehouse produced four or five videos, though he viewed them as little more than side projects. He assumed his audience was limited to the eight or twelve people in his local Sunday school class. However, the digital reach of his small project was far greater than he imagined. A year later, a viewer who had seen his stop-motion work online reached out to collaborate on a LEGO-based Easter story. Recognizing the potential of this unique medium, a Christian nonprofit stepped in to offer a partnership, providing a platform to distribute his videos to a global audience.

The idea "really excited" him. He realized his passion for LEGO was a unique way to unlock his gifts to share the gospel: "I put a huge amount of effort into that animation because I could see the value it could have in the wider Christian community." Remarkably, the Easter project was used in over 1,200 churches and its success would lead to the launch of Go Chatter Studios, an independent nonprofit that creates Bible stories in LEGO stop-motion animation.

At first glance, a LEGO project might seem like an unusual church activity. After all, LEGO is simply a collection of plastic bricks—yet it gives individuals the power to create something from nothing. This is the heart of freestyle evangelism: empowering people to use their unique gifts and imagination to creatively express their faith.

Although using LEGO might seem like a departure from formal church customs, it serves as a powerful universal language—a bridge that connects people across generations. Because these bricks evoke fond memories and rekindle the emotional joy of childhood, they create an immediate point of connection with their childhoods. As Whitehouse observes, LEGO "engages such a wide range of people." People discover the gospel in a way that is so endearing that the message feels less like a lecture and more like a retelling of a story through innocent amazement found in a familiar childhood toy. Whitehouse says, "When people see one of our animations, they're immediately drawn in—just because it's LEGO. It grabs their attention, and then we're sharing a Bible story and the gospel with them through this medium they're already interested in."

LEGO serves as a common ground where divisions are bridged on a platform where every piece belongs. In a world where imagination and construction are the starting points, Whitehouse discovered that evangelism through LEGO is uniquely unburdened. It is free from the perception of pushing an agenda or imposing a worldview. Instead, it invites the viewer into a shared creative space, allowing the story of the gospel to be heard without the immediate friction of cultural or religious barriers. "LEGO is a neutral, content-neutral medium," Whitehouse says, "so it draws in people outside the faith and gets them excited about the Bible stories we create."

Through Go Chatter Studios, Whitehouse makes his videos accessible free of charge on YouTube, Instagram, and TikTok. This ensures parents can easily use them to introduce family devotions—turning routine screen time into a springboard for biblical discussion. For church leaders, these videos serve as a versatile resource for children's ministries, Vacation Bible School, and Sunday services. By providing a concrete visual for complex theological concepts, the LEGO medium captures the attention of young listeners who might otherwise struggle with more abstract teaching.

Maddie Tucker and Blessing Boxes

We don't usually expect an eight-year-old to organize church events, but Maddie Tucker isn't your typical third grader. She helped bring the viral Blessing Box movement to her church in Collinsville, Oklahoma, placing a red food pantry right at the edge of the church parking lot. The sign on the side says it all: "Take what you need, Leave what you can, Always be blessed."[67] It serves as a round-the-clock resource where neighbors can quietly find a meal or drop off a donation for those in need.

In 2022, Maddie and her friends expanded the mission by adding a Pet Blessing Box alongside the original pantry. Designed to look like a miniature church—complete with a cross and a glass door—the wooden structure offers free pet supplies to anyone in need. Beyond standard cat and dog food, the box stays stocked with treats, leashes, collars, and even the occasional pet bed.

Maddie wasn't done. "One day as I was singing in church," she says in an interview with a local news station, "I like to read and I got a little bored so I thought of a book box. I just wanted it to be kinda like a library but you don't have to return the book or pay for them." She drew up a blueprint of what the Library Blessings

Box would look like and presented the idea to the church board.

Maddie's mother said, "She went to some of the people in the church and gave them her ideas and they thought it was a great idea and so they got behind her and everyone worked together in the community to make it happen." When children are truly heard and given the space to lead, their capabilities often exceed our expectations. While they are usually taught to follow rules and defer to adults, imagine the possibilities if they were instead encouraged to take the initiative.

When asked about the project, Pastor Nathan Mattox was clear: "The ideas are all from the children."[68] He noted that Maddie even presented her vision for the third box directly to a church committee. Meadowcreek United Methodist was elastic enough to take a child's ideas seriously, fostering a culture of genuine innovation. Through this, Maddie discovered that her church didn't just listen—it valued her enough to support her in making a community-wide impact. When churches embrace children's leadership without fear, they open new, unexpected pathways to the world around them.

Cafeteria Worker and Her Passion

A local news segment went to a local high school cafeteria to document the demanding work of feeding 2,200 students on a regular basis. The profile showed the physical toll of the early hours: cleaning the industrial cooking equipment, preparing the massive kettles, and transferring heavy sacks of food to the prepping stations. The reporter highlighted the relentless mad rush to prep thousands of meals before the first bell signals the start of the day.

The news crew captured the frantic energy of the midday rush, where students practically sprinted to the cafeteria the moment the bell rang. Cameras followed a human conveyor belt of teenagers moving along the rails with metal trays. Behind the counter, the staff served one student after another without a second's rest—handing out hot meals while others scrambled to restock the serving stations. In the kitchen, the back-of-house crew was a blur of motion, constantly chopping ingredients, boiling pasta, and sliding fresh trays into the ovens.

Amid the roar of the lunchroom, the reporter asked a staff member about the relentless pressure of the pace. Her response was entirely unexpected. "It's a privilege to help feed students with bright futures," she explained. "I'm so grateful."[69] Struck by her perspective, the reporter leaned in, asking her to elaborate on why she felt that way. She smiled and replied, "We're like moms to them. That makes me happy."

In a world where many complain about their work, the reporter was curious about her joy and pressed her further. "If we didn't feel this way, it would just be a routine task," she explained. "But we do it for the students. That's what drives us." While some might see a cafeteria role as merely a means to a paycheck, for her, the job wasn't about the wage—it was the deep satisfaction that she is making a profound difference. Beyond the repetitive tasks, she sees a mission: contributing to the growth of young people year after year. Her work was a personal calling to nurture her community through its youth. "I'd still like to understand everyone's likes and dislikes better," she added with a smile, "but I haven't quite managed that yet."

While the world sees only a cafeteria worker, she sees a passion that adds deep meaning to her life. By embracing what she loves, her daily tasks are transformed into a mission that makes her feel alive. These internal drivers—whether found in a job, a family, or a craft—give us a sense of purpose, elevating our existence beyond the mundane and the routine.

Freestyle evangelism is about releasing the existing passions that members already have. It shouldn't feel like they are doing ministry; rather, they are doing what they love. This paradigm suggests that church growth shouldn't feel like doing a program or doing a prearranged activity, but a natural by-product of releasing members to be innovators. When an individual's passions are affirmed, their message becomes authentic, unrehearsed, and magnetic. If church members approach their callings with the same joy as the cafeteria worker, they won't need to be prompted—they will eagerly find their own ways to show Christ to the world.

Misha Raichura and Youth Mental Health

Never before has a generation been so linked to others through digital platforms, yet felt so profoundly alone. Despite being the most connected generation in history, Gen Z is frequently labeled the loneliest generation. The data paints a stark picture: Research from the Walton Family Foundation shows that 42 percent of Gen Z struggle with depression—nearly double the rate of adults over 25 percent. Meanwhile a study by Harmony Healthcare IT found that 61 percent have been medically diagnosed with an anxiety disorder.[70]

In a 2023 report, the CDC revealed startling findings among twelve-to-seventeen-year-olds. In thirty years of collecting this data, Kathleen Ethier, the director of Adolescent and School Health, said, "We've never seen this kind of devastating, consistent findings. There's no question young people are telling us they are in crisis. The data really call on us to act."[71] The data revealed that 42 percent of high school students felt persistently sad or hopeless—a record-breaking rate at the time. Ethier warns: "Young people are experiencing a level of distress that calls on us to act with urgency and compassion."[72]

While older adults are deeply concerned about young people, they often find themselves at a loss to understand the lived experience of the first digital-native generation. They struggle to grasp the relentless pressure of being always on. While teens are constantly connected, they inhabit a world where they can't simply shut down their devices or keep their private lives to themselves. This digital immersion breeds a specific kind of anxiety—one that offers no escape and makes it impossible to fully detach.

In 2018, school superintendents in Johnson County, Kansas, launched the Zero Reasons Why campaign in response to a heartbreaking rise in teen suicides. While initiated as a school program, the campaign's success rests on its peer-to-peer mission—driven by student leaders like Misha Raichura of Blue Valley High School. By 2026, the movement has expanded significantly, with hundreds of teen advocates gathering annually at the state capitol to dismantle mental health stigma. The campaign's core power lies in making teens feel understood rather than judged; instead of the clinical feeling of "seeking help," these interactions often feel like simply spending time together, removing the shame often associated with mental health struggles.

A high school student said, "I think they're way more comfortable talking to someone their age about it and not having to hear, 'What you are doing is bad.'"[73] Creating a baseline of understanding is crucial to drawing them out of isolation. Guarded feelings are more likely to be lowered when a teen realizes a peer truly understands the same daily pressures they face. The unique struggles of their generation are what make fellow teens the most relatable people capable of translating for one another. It is the quiet and discreet nature of teen distress that makes it so hard for even the most willing adults to notice a problem. However, Misha Raichura has become an expert at reading between the lines to find the hidden signals of a peer in distress. "Usually they wouldn't use the word 'depressed' or 'take my own life,'" Raichura said. "It would be more like 'I'm so done with this, I'm just going to end everything.' Or 'thank you for being a good friend, while it lasted.'"[74] Even without a college degree or formal training in counseling, Raichura has learned to decode the subtle cues of her peers effectively and hear the silent calls for help.

In the local church context, transformation begins when leadership realizes that its best candidates for revival are already sitting in the pews. These individuals are the native experts of their own subcultures. However, when an institution prioritizes precedent over organic energy, it unintentionally stifles the very Spirit moving its members. The overreliance on church rules and a fear of the unknown handcuff those who desire to live out an authentic faith—sending a message that church regulations matter more than individuals' passions. When people are forced to wait for permission that never arrives, they eventually lose the fire they started with.

CLOSING THOUGHTS

Our world has far more moving parts than it once did. In 1960, watching television meant choosing between three major networks. Today, a global satellite plan offers over five hundred channels—and that doesn't even include the dozens of streaming services providing a vast library of content at our fingertips. Life was simpler in 1960, and churches dealt with fewer complexities. Today, the "one-size-fits-all" approach is no longer effective. Modern society is defined by a deep diversity of backgrounds, needs, and spiritual pain points that a single congregation—no matter how large—cannot possibly cover on its own.

We no longer live in one cohesive group; instead, society has fragmented into a mosaic of divergent interests. We inhabit hundreds of separate worlds orbiting different niche communities, socioeconomic strata, and distinct worldviews. In such a landscape, a local church cannot realistically be everything to everyone. However, by empowering its members to focus on their specific spheres of influence, it can still make a deep and lasting impact within the community.

Ordinary church members are the vital link between the sanctuary and the neighborhood. They are the everyday folks who work, shop, and live their lives in the same town. As hardworking people who spend their days in the area, they stay in touch with the local concerns that truly matter—making them the most authentic witnesses to the community's needs.

Using the freestyle model, congregations can create a framework for laypeople to bridge the gap between the church and the local community. Freestyle is about meeting people where they are and releasing them as they are, enkindled by the Holy Spirit. When ordinary people are empowered to freestyle, they bring a level of authenticity and creativity that formal programs can never imitate. Our pews are filled with individuals—like the cafeteria worker—who find deep joy and meaning in their daily roles, yet their potential often remains unnoticed and unconnected.

As the stories in this chapter illustrate, the capacity for innovation lives within every person. However, no one is meant to innovate in isolation; they need the church's embrace and active support to pursue what they are truly passionate about. For a vision to become a reality, a congregation must walk side by side with its members, offering the scaffolding they need to build. When an enkindled soul succeeds, the entire church body enjoys the fruits of that labor. The spiritual ripples do not stop at the sanctuary doors—they spread outward to touch and transform the whole neighborhood.

6

The Holy Spirit as Enkindler

Earlier in chapter 4, we see Peter and John hauled before the Sanhedrin, a body of about seventy-one members that is made up of the country's leading experts and high-level religious leaders. The apostles found themselves facing the full weight of the political and religious establishment as the rulers, elders, and scribes joined forces with Annas the high priest, Caiaphas, John, and Alexander, and "all who were of the high-priestly family" to demand an account of their deeds (Acts 4: 5–6).

The apostles and the Sanhedrin could not have been more different. Peter and John wore unbleached and unrefined linen, while the luxury of the council's multicolored robes and embroidered headwear acted as a symbol of their office and prestige. While the air in the council chamber was thick with the scent of expensive incense, Peter and John's tunics still smelled of salt wind and fish.

Peter and John were lifelong fishermen. Neither of them had the chance to sit at the feet of great teachers to receive rabbinical training, instructions in the interpretations of the Law, or education in the traditions of the elders. They were "unlearned and ignorant," or *idiotes*, in terms of rabbinical learning, but the people on the council were completely caught off guard by what they said. Peter addressed the council directly:

"Rulers of the people and elders. If we are questioned today because of a good deed done to someone who was sick and are asked how this man has been healed, let it be known to all of you, and to all the people of Israel, that this man is standing before you in good health by the name of Jesus Christ of Nazareth, whom you crucified, whom God raised from the dead. This Jesus is 'the stone that was rejected by you, the builders; it has become the cornerstone.' There is salvation in no one else, for there is no other name under heaven given among mortals by which we must be saved." (Acts 4:8–13)

Peter and John were men of the sea, far more comfortable with fishing nets than theological debates. Yet, they spoke with a depth that baffled the religious elite. The Sanhedrin was left "amazed," unable to reconcile the apostles' lack of formal training with the power of their message (Acts 4:13).

How was it possible that men from a small fishing village were able to speak with such theological authority? Verse 8 provides the answer: They were "filled with the Holy Spirit." Peter himself might have been surprised by the words flowing from his mouth, perhaps recalling the moment Jesus warned them of this exact situation: "When they bring you before the synagogues, the rulers, and the authorities, do not worry about how you are to defend yourselves or what you are to say; for the Holy Spirit will teach you at that very hour what you ought to say" (Luke 12:12).

Even though the idea of Jesus being the Messiah wasn't new to the Sanhedrin as they had heard of it before, but there was something about the way it was said this time that made it feel much more unsettling. Peter's words left the council blindsided and reeling as he declared, "This Jesus is, 'the stone that was rejected by you, the builders; it has become the cornerstone'" (Acts 4:11). Peter was quoting from Psalm 118:22, but it wasn't the first time the members of the council had heard this verse used against them. Jesus had leveled those exact words at them once before.

In Luke 20:17–18, Jesus asked the scribes and chief priests, "What then does this text mean: 'The stone that the builders rejected has become the cornerstone? Everyone who falls on that stone will be broken to pieces; and it will crush anyone on whom it falls.'" They were completely caught off guard because they realized that the story Jesus just told was actually highlighting their own rejection of God. They "realized that he told this parable against them." Their anger burned so hot that "they wanted to lay hands on him at that very hour," but they restrained themselves only because "they feared the people" (Luke 20:19).

It is likely that many members of the Sanhedrin remembered this grave insult firsthand. Some may have even been in the crowd when Jesus first leveled it against them. Interestingly, the religious elite interrogated both Jesus and Peter with the exact same question regarding their authority and legitimacy. "Tell us," they demanded of Jesus, "by what authority are you doing these things? Who is it who gave you this authority?" (Luke 20:2). To Peter and John, they asked, "By what power or by what name did you do this?" (Acts 4:7).

One can only imagine the council's unease as Peter threw that same Scripture back at them. Previously, they had to endure the insult from Jesus; now, they were forced to hear his followers use the exact same argument against them. Jesus was a one-of-a-kind speaker they found impossible to trap or prove wrong, but Peter and John were just ordinary guys with regular day jobs.

When enkindled by the Holy Spirit, an ordinary individual can fearlessly stand up to the most powerful people in the land and say irrefutable words. Because these individuals have been enkindled, they find it impossible to sit still, and they discover a hidden strength to act in new and different ways. Not only do they have a strong internal drive, but that very fire is what gives them the passion to persevere through challenging situations and finish what they started.

The very thing that makes a person enkindled—their enthusiastic fire to make a difference in the world—is often exactly what makes them a challenge for a church to manage. These individuals frequently arrive without a road map, driven solely by an intense desire to lead the charge in their specific calling. To thrive, church leadership must shift its culture: moving beyond simple "permission" toward an active partnership in discovery. The church functions best when it operates as a creative laboratory, a space where members aren't just filling roles, but are actively assisting one another in refining and realizing their God-given visions.

Philip and the Ethiopian Church

In Ethiopia, there are rock-hewn churches that are unlike any church structure you have ever seen. While we usually imagine buildings rising from the ground up, these were created in reverse: They were carved from the top down, straight into the living bedrock. Meticulously chiseled over eight hundred years ago, they remain one of humanity's greatest architectural feats. Standing at the edge of the trench, a visitor realizes they are standing on the very ground that serves as the ceiling for the worshippers below.

Far from being tourist destinations, these rock-hewn sanctuaries remain active centers of worship, hosting the same sacred liturgies they did eight centuries ago. Streams of devotees in traditional white *shamas* still descend into the stone trenches to offer their prayers, songs, and worship to the Lord. Ethiopia holds the rare distinction of becoming a Christian state in the early fourth century while the Roman Empire was still officially pagan and persecuting Christians.

Remarkably, Ethiopian tradition traces the nation's conversion to Christianity back to Philip's interaction with a court official on the road from Jerusalem to Gaza. This was no ordinary traveler; he was the high-ranking eunuch in charge of the entire treasury of the Candance, queen of the Ethiopians. As Philip ran up to the official's chariot, he heard him reading aloud from the prophet Isaiah: "Like a sheep he was led to the slaughter, and like a lamb silent before its shearer, so he does not open his mouth. In his humiliation justice was denied him. Who can describe his generation? For his life is taken away from the earth" (Acts 8:32–33).

The Ethiopian was particularly struck by this unnamed person in the passage, sparking a deep curiosity about who the prophet was describing. Looking at Philip, he asked, "About whom, may I ask you, does the prophet say this, about himself or about someone else?" (Acts 8:34). Beginning with that very passage in Isaiah, Philip guided the official through the Scriptures, unpacking their deeper meaning and ultimately revealing how the prophecies were fulfilled in Jesus. Philip "proclaimed to him the good news about Jesus" (Acts 8:35).

A spark of faith was ignited in the Ethiopian's soul as he chose to believe in Christ right then and there. Then, the Ethiopian spots a body of water, such as a fountain or stream, but large enough for both of them to go "down into the water" (v. 36). The two men went down into the water together, and Philip baptized him. While the Scriptures provide no further mention of the official after this encounter, we can imagine him returning home with a heart full of the stories he experienced on the road. Historical tradition suggests he became an early evangelist, using his authority and prestige to plant the seeds of Christianity deep into Ethiopian soil.

Philip's encounter with the Ethiopian official is a familiar story in Acts, but how did Philip end up in the middle of nowhere, traveling with a group of complete strangers? The answer lies in a specific, divine nudge. God led him with the instruction: "Get up and go toward the south to the road that goes down from Jerusalem and Gaza" (Act 8:26). Without hesitation, Philip "got up and went" (v. 27). Notice that God chose not to provide any further details; Philip was simply told to "get up and go" in a certain direction.

Imagine Philip's situation. Joining the caravan, he likely had no idea what to do next. Philip would have walked alongside a very long train of camels and people of different political and economic standings. For example, Philip would have caught sight of armed guards protecting the caravan; cooks and servants to prepare meals along the way; scribes and attendants managing official affairs; and chariots with their drivers.

Of all the chariots in the caravan, the Holy Spirit singled out one to Philip: "Go over to this chariot and join it" (Acts 8:29). What's interesting is the Holy Spirit's vague instruction to simply "join it." There was no strategy for after he reached the chariot, no script for what to say. Just go. Even though Philip was clearly being guided, many would find it unsettling to be left so in the dark about the end goal. He was forced to navigate the situation one step at a time.

By leaving the details to discernment, the Holy Spirit invited Philip to be a creative innovator—to step into the unknown and partner in an unfolding plan. This moment reveals a willingness to trust the Spirit's guidance without having a road map. Philip obeyed, "running up" to the chariot to find a man deeply immersed in the Scriptures, searching for a truth he couldn't yet grasp. While reading Isaiah, the man was stuck, unsure if the prophet wrote of himself or another.

At that point, Philip understood. He took the lead and began to speak, using his knowledge of the Scriptures, to introduce Christ to the Ethiopian. Having spent so much time by the Savior's side, Philip didn't just recite sermons; he recounted the small, kind remarks Jesus made in their daily life together. By allowing Philip to be himself, God empowered him to speak in a way only he could. That single decision to obey ignited a fire that would eventually transform an entire nation—a legacy that still thrives in Ethiopia today.

Ananias

Though mentioned only briefly, Ananias left a monumental mark on Christian history. He proves that an ordinary believer can spark massive change simply by heeding the Spirit's call. Yet, his task was anything but easy; in fact, he feared for his life. News had reached the Christians in Damascus of the brutal persecution in Jerusalem, and Ananias knew exactly who was coming for them.

The man spearheading the persecution was Saul, and he was now headed to Damascus with one goal: to dismantle the church. His reputation preceded him, striking terror into the hearts of the local believers. "Saul, still breathing threats and murder against the disciples of the Lord, went to the high priest and asked him for letters to the synagogues at Damascus, so that if he found any who belonged to the Way, men or women, he might bring them bound to Jerusalem" (Acts 9:1–2).

Christians were on the edge, in fear of being shackled and dragged off in irons to Jerusalem. The forced march to Jerusalem would have taken about ten days. However, the threat never materialized, because "a light from heaven [suddenly] flashed around" Saul on the road to Damascus (Acts 9:3). Saul collapsed to the ground and heard a voice, "Saul, Saul, why do you persecute me?" Saul asked, "Who are you, Lord?" A reply followed: "I am Jesus, whom you are persecuting. But get up and enter the city, and you will be told what you are to do" (Acts 9:4–6).

The experience didn't just terrify Saul; it left him completely blind. Saul's companions assisted him by leading him by hand into the city. At this time, Ananias saw a vision in which the Lord said to him, "Get up and go to the street called Straight, and at the house of Judas look for a man of Tarsus named Saul. At this moment he is praying, and he has seen in a vision a man named Ananias come in and lay his hands on him so that he might regain his sight" (Acts 9:11–12).

Ananias was afraid. "Lord, I have heard from many about this man, how much evil he has done to your saints in Jerusalem; and here he has authority from the chief priests to bind all who invoke your name" (Acts 9:13–14). The biblical narrative offers no explanation for why God chose Ananias, other than his quiet faithfulness.

Knowing Saul's violent reputation, Ananias had every reason to fear. Yet, setting aside his apprehension, he did exactly what was asked of him. He found the house of Judas on the street called Straight, knocked, and entered. By addressing him as "Brother Saul," Ananias showed a remarkable, godly affection—choosing to see a brother in the man in spite of all the evil he had inflicted on the Christians. "The Lord Jesus, who appeared to you on your way here, has sent me so that you may regain your sight and be filled with the Holy Spirit" (Acts 9:17).

Could God have restored Saul's vision without Ananias? Absolutely—but God invited him into the process. Similarly, God graciously chooses to include ordinary individuals to be part of the unfolding. In time, Saul (who would take on his Roman name Paul when he transitioned to Gentile ministry) would become one of history's most significant figures. Yet, it was Ananias who played a small, critical role that made it all possible.

The Holy Spirit continues to speak to us today, quietly nudging individuals toward the next step for their church and community. The real question is: Will the rest of the church be open to it? Leadership must be ready to discern and catch the spark of a new idea or initiative that God has placed in someone's heart. The

Spirit is constantly moving, but will the church pivot when a new wind begins to blow through the congregation?

Cornelius

Going to meet Cornelius in Acts 10 was no small feat for Peter. He knew his decision would draw fire from the other disciples, who later demanded: "Why did you go to uncircumcised men and eat with them?" (Acts 11:3). Peter was being called to account for breaking an established custom; Jewish tradition at the time strictly prohibited entering the home of a Gentile like Cornelius, the Roman centurion stationed in Caesarea.

By heeding the Holy Spirit, Peter defied custom and reshaped the very identity of the church. While praying on a rooftop, Peter "fell into a trance" and saw a marvelous vision: "the heaven opening and something like a large sheet coming down, being lowered to the ground by its four corners. In it were all kinds of four-footed creatures and reptiles and birds of the air. Then he heard a voice saying, 'Get up, Peter; kill and eat.' But Peter said, 'By no means, Lord; for I have never eaten anything that is profane or unclean.' The voice said to him again, a second time, 'What God has made clean, you must not call profane'" (Acts 10:11–15). This vision repeats itself "three times"—a repetition that surely echoed the moment Jesus questioned Peter's love three times by the sea, transforming his past dismay into a new commission (John 21:15–17).

This time, however, Peter didn't waver, believing fully in the Holy Spirit's message, even though it went directly against long-held beliefs. After the vision, visitors arrived at the house. They told Peter, "[Cornelius] was directed by a holy angel to send for you to come to his house and to hear what you have to say" (Acts 10:22). Peter hesitated, and the Holy Spirit interjected. Peter said, "The Spirit told me to go with [Cornelius's men] and not to make a distinction between them and us" (Acts 11:12). Peter took "six brothers" with him the next day to Caesarea.

When Peter arrived, he was very direct: "So when I was sent for, I came without objection. Now may I ask why you sent for me?" (Acts 10:29). Cornelius replied, "Four days ago at this very hour, at three o'clock, I was praying in my house when suddenly a man in dazzling clothes stood before me" (v. 30). Cornelius proceeded to explain how he was told to bring Peter to his home and listen to what he had to say.

Peter was flabbergasted; he thought back to what had happened the day before. Just as Peter's vision ended, Cornelius's men arrived at the door looking for him. Peter realized the impeccable timing wasn't a coincidence, and the weight of the realization hit him when he traveled to meet Cornelius. In the vision, God instructed Peter three times, "What God has made clean, you must not call profane" (Acts 10:15). In the NIV, it reads: "Do not call anything impure that God has made clean."

As Peter recoiled at the threshold of the centurion's home, God's warning echoed in his mind, directly challenging everything he thought he knew about holiness. "I truly understand that God shows no partiality," declared a joyful Peter in front of Cornelius and the Gentiles that assembled before him (Acts 10:34). Listening to Peter tell the gospel to a group of Gentiles must have been a surreal experience for him.

Peter began to tell them about Jesus from the moment the Savior first called his name on the Sea of Galilee, to witnessing miracles, watching the gruesome crucifixion, and finally dining with him after the resurrection. He spoke as an eyewitness, drawing on a firsthand experience that only a disciple could provide. Just as Peter finished speaking about "everyone who believes in him receives forgiveness of sins through his name," the room suddenly combusted with holy fire. "While Peter was still speaking, the Holy Spirit fell upon all who heard the word" (Acts 10:44). Peter's Jewish companions were in disbelief over what just occurred. "The circumcised believers who had come with Peter were astounded that the gift of the Holy Spirit had been poured out even on the Gentiles" (v.45).

In that moment, Peter abandoned his long-held assumptions and immediately pivoted to the Holy Spirit's leading. Peter asked his companions, "Can anyone withhold the water for baptizing these people who have received the Holy Spirit just as we have?" (Acts 10:47). Seeing no distinction between himself and the Romans, Peter "ordered them to be baptized in the name of Jesus Christ" (v. 48).

Upon his return to Jerusalem, Peter was met not with celebration, but with a cross-examination from believers who were deeply skeptical of his actions (Acts 11:2). Peter recounted the entire sequence of events—the vision, the Spirit's command, and the enkindling at Cornelius's house. His critics were silenced, eventually moving from suspicion to praising God for opening the door to the Gentiles. Peter said, "If then God gave them the same gift that he gave us when we believed in the Lord Jesus Christ, who was I that I could hinder God?" (Acts 11:17). Because of Peter's testimony, their narrow view of the movement was shattered—

transforming the church from a local sect into a global mission. "They were silenced. And they praised God, saying, 'Then God has given even to the Gentiles the repentance that leads to life" (Acts 11:18). Imagine the possibilities when churches listen to the leading of the Holy Spirit!

CLOSING THOUGHTS

While we have many resources, tools, and programs to help churches grow, the Holy Spirit remains the only spark capable of truly igniting a congregation. To see revitalization, we must shift our focus from human-developed strategies to an active, guiding partnership with the Holy Spirit.

Currently, the church struggles to prove its relevance in contemporary society. Denominations are working hard to bridge the widening gap between formal traditions and modern life, yet many congregations find it difficult to let go of a past culture that prized conformity. The challenge now is to move toward a more elastic church culture—one that can stretch and adapt without losing its soul.

In the past, the church has relied on predictable agendas and data-driven outcomes to reach the unchurched—but the old methods are losing their touch. Real progress happens when we realize our role isn't to manage the Holy Spirit's influence, but to get out of the way. Instead of controlling the process, we must invite and champion the unique, enkindled fire that the Spirit is already lighting in the hearts of people.

True vitality isn't about finding the perfect program to boost a church's profile. To become relevant again, we must return our focus to the Holy Spirit—the primary catalyst for any living congregation. We often call the Spirit "Helper," "Counselor," and "Advocate," and the church has never needed that help more than now. In a world of endless distractions, a Spirit-led church offers an unmistakable authenticity. The unchurched aren't looking for more religion; they are searching for a genuine connection with the Living God.

A Spirit-led church is flexible enough to pause and seriously consider new ideas, even when they challenge the status quo. Because the Holy Spirit provides unique gifts to every person at their specific station in life, a congregation's role is to celebrate these enkindled souls and help them find their purpose. This shift transforms church members into stakeholders—moving them from the sidelines of spectators into a "cloud of witnesses" (Hebrews 12:1) who are intimately invested in the growth of everyone around them.

In a world where people crave realness, the Holy Spirit delivers authenticity that cannot be manufactured or rehearsed. While the church often feels overwhelmed by contemporary challenges that didn't exist in the past, its inability to respond often stems from an inward focus on self-preservation. However, when we release enkindled souls, the focus shifts outward to a world in need. A Spirit-led church remains forever relevant because those enkindled souls are uniquely equipped to serve their specific communities in ways that no program could ever reproduce.

Conclusion

Looking back on years of church life, Brooke Knoop asks a very blunt question on the *reChurch* podcast: "Is this it?"[75] She found herself wondering if a predictable routine was truly the peak of the faith experience. "I come [to church] every Sunday," Knoop says, "and you sit down and it's three songs, tithe, and offerings, you know, and a thirty- to forty-five-minute message, and then you shake some people's hands on the way out and tell them, 'Have a good week. See you next week.'"

Knoop describes a church that has traded its spark for the safety of institutional identity, choosing predictable patterns over the risk of an uncharted path. She questions whether the church even realizes it is fading into irrelevance by clinging so tightly to tradition. "Is this it? It can't be it," she says, her disillusionment clear.

Her growth feels stunted—not by a lack of faith, but by a lack of elasticity in a system resistant to change. Her final question is a haunting one: "Is this all that I get to do in the kingdom of God until Jesus returns?"

Knoop gives voice to a widespread spiritual longing: the desire to move past surface-level religion and into an unfiltered, undeniable relationship with God. Authenticity is the relational glue that binds us to God and to one another. Without the deployment of our deeply personal gifts, faith becomes a sterile exercise rather than a lived reality. When believers are forced to suppress their true calling, their religious life and their God-given potential never meet—leading to a spiritual "quiet-quitting" that leaves the church hollow.

While "quiet-quitting" began as a workplace trend—a desire to step back and focus on life outside the office—it has now been adopted by Christians. Nicole Nuehring is a prime example; she describes a slow withdrawal from a place that was once her "anchor," but "it's not anymore."[76] She observes her peers doing the same—slipping away without a fuss, making no noise as they quietly exit.

The church was once a dominant pillar in society, but it now occupies the margins of the postmodern mind. The constant stream of notifications and digital media, combined with the demands of work and family obligations, has made church one of many priorities. Rather than reacting with frustration or escalating the matter against the church, believers like Nuehring quietly accept the church's diminished relevance and turn to other options for a more personal spiritual challenge. With a sense of resignation, Nuehring says, "It was easier to quiet-quit."

During a session at an evangelism conference, I invited the participants to move beyond the statistics and discuss the practical challenges that numerical decline is having on their congregations. The vast majority of those in the audience held pastoral roles, meaning they didn't need to think about it in a theoretical way; they were living in it. One person made an excellent observation that seemed to capture what is happening in the broader society: "Young people, they are interested in participating but not becoming a part of church itself."

This trend of unlinking from organized religion is backed by decades of data showing a steady drop in weekly attendance. Yet, thinning pews don't necessarily mean a loss of belief; many keep their personal faith intact. The spiritual landscape remains vibrant, fueled by a desire for connection and service that is as strong as ever.

These individuals aren't "walking away" from God; according to sociologist Josh Packard, they are often leaving the institutional church to save their faith. Packard identifies them as the "Dones"—people who leave not because of a loss of belief, but because institutional obligations have become overwhelming.[77] They want meaningful ministry but grow disillusioned when their energy is spent merely keeping the organizational structures running. "Top-down hierarchy of worship- and ministry-planning not only alienated those committed volunteers and staff from doing church work, but it also alienated them spiritually."[78] Participation in congregations is "still lagging," according to David Brubaker, a professor specializing in the study of religious organizations. "Congregants may show up on a Saturday or Sunday but are less apt to jump in and help," Brubaker says. However, they will stay and engage, he adds, if they "find meaning and connection."[79]

At an Impasse

In *Who Moved My Cheese?* Hem and Haw continued to return to the empty room long after the cheese had vanished, convinced it would somehow reappear. Haw finally realizes that "when he had been afraid to change he had been holding on to the illusion of Old Cheese that was no longer there."[80] For Hem, however, the thought of leaving for the unknown was just too much. "I like here," Hem declares, "It's comfortable. It's what I know."[81] He had become so set in his ways that he chose the safety of a barren room over the risk of a new life, ultimately staying exactly where he was.

During a conference, I asked the audience of pastors, church officials, and active laypeople to describe what a church in decline looks like when it is slowly losing its energy and members. As the conversation continued, a consistent theme started to emerge. I typed the first comment, "Uncomfortable with change," so that it appeared on the big screen for everyone to see. Next, another person added, "Concerned about legacy." The next person chimed in with, "Longer in church, harder to have a new perspective." Despite the fact that these individuals came from all over, they were describing their struggles in identical ways.

Even as attendance figures drop, church leaders find it difficult to pivot to a new direction. Breaking away from "the way we've always done it" feels like a gamble they aren't ready to take. They struggle with the same paralysis as Hem: "What if there is no Cheese out there? Or even if there is, what if we never find it?" In a way, Hem's anxiety is logical. What if the search for cheese outside our familiar ways is a wild goose chase? What if we end up right back where we started, only more exhausted? These fears make the empty, familiar room feel safer than the unknown path to survival. A lot of churches think this way, deciding that staying with what they know is better than investing in something unknown. At the same time, these same congregations are left wondering why they can't seem to draw in new members or bridge the gap with the younger generation.

Growing Our Congregations

It is time to question the assumptions we have long followed. Churches have turned to strategic expansion plans, like copying what large successful churches are doing or adopting the latest revitalization trend, that are no longer effective. In addition, outdated assumptions built on patterns that once defined the way we practiced church growth often prevent innovation. Congregations turn to outreach strategies that come with step-by-step instructions, hoping that the latest model will be effective.

The central premise of this book is simple: The innovators we've been looking for are already here—they are the people sitting in our pews. A major barrier to church growth is the flawed assumption that regular members aren't equipped for ministry because they lack formal training. We have bought into the idea that only experts can drive change, mistakenly believing that ordinary people don't fit the description of a leader.

This book challenges our deeply held assumptions by arguing the counterintuitive: The people in the pews are often the ones best equipped for the mission. They know their neighbors' hearts and understand the local struggles far better than an outside expert ever could. When ordinary people are enkindled, their everyday backgrounds become their greatest assets. The Holy Spirit takes their ordinary lives and makes them extraordinary—instilling them with the confidence that *they* are the "someone else" God has been looking for.

God's enkindling provides the momentum needed to break through our hardened walls. These enkindled souls become innovators, instinctively carving pathways for their newfound vision. If the Holy Spirit provides the spark, then human passion is the fuel that drives them forward. When enkindled, an ordinary person is compelled to act—driven by a restless need to fill a gap in their neighborhood or stand with those who are struggling. It is vital to realize that laypeople don't need a title or special training to begin; a regular person with a regular job is more than enough. Their passion is raw and honest, making it both authentic and magnetic. This enkindling can happen to anyone, at any time, for the "wind blows where it chooses" (John 3:8).

When others see an ordinary person acting with such passion, it becomes contagious. The authenticity of that experience inspires everyone around them, allowing the enkindling to spill over and ignite holy fires in the most unexpected places. This is how true movements begin—not with a top-down agenda, but with a single individual who decided to act on the Holy Spirit's inspiration.

However, the greatest barrier to this move is often a congregation's comfort level. Are we truly ready to support innovations we have never seen before? It is far too easy for a church to extinguish a new spark with hesitation or disapproval. Holy fires must be tended if they are to stay lit and grow strong. When a congregation rejoices with its enkindled people, it helps them see that their unique gifts aren't just personal interests—they are vital tools being put into action for the Lord.

Haw Finds New Cheese

Haw nervously stepped out of Cheese Station C and into the unknown. Though fear filled his heart, he kept moving anyway. He had no guarantee of success, but he carried something more vital: the willingness to be wrong. He realized that finding a new path required a mind open enough to leave the old one behind. Despite his nerves, Haw embraced the challenge, finally breaking through the invisible walls of his own making.

The journey wasn't easy. Despite his efforts, Haw found only scattered crumbs, leaving him discouraged and defeated. Yet, he chose to keep moving. In that persistence, he had a powerful realization: The movement itself was the reward. Through the cycle of moving, failing, and learning, his outlook shifted. Even without a full supply of cheese, his confidence grew. He was no longer a victim of his circumstances but an explorer who embraced the unknown. Spencer Johnson writes, "You can believe that a change will harm you and resist it. Or you can believe that finding New Cheese will help you and embrace the change."[82]

Stepping into the unknown wasn't easy, but the maze became less intimidating once Haw stopped worrying about what could go wrong and focused on the journey itself. In the past, reaching a dead end would have left him overwhelmed with frustration; now, he simply turns around and tries a new path. He has realized that a dead end isn't a permanent failure—it's just a sign to find a different route.

One day, Haw turned a corner and stopped in his tracks. Before him lay Cheese Station N: a vast ocean of cheese that seemed to go on forever. It was a staggering upgrade from Cheese Station C, with an assortment of varieties he hadn't even known existed. As he wondered if he was dreaming, he spotted his old friends, Sniff and Scurry. They didn't look surprised to see him; they simply waved, their full bellies proving they had been enjoying this new place for quite some time.

As Haw savored the new varieties, he felt a wave of gratitude—but his heart was heavy for Hem. Somewhere in the dark maze, his friend remained bitter, waiting for a past that wasn't coming back. Their story is a stark cautionary tale: two people who started in the same position but reached vastly different ends because of the decisions they made. One embraced the discomfort of the unknown; the other clung to the comfort of the familiar. It offers an important lesson about the consequences of not moving out of our limitations. At the end of the book, however, we learn that there is hope for Hem, but we don't know for sure what exactly happens to him. The ambiguous ending is deliberate; by placing Hem's dilemma in the hands of the reader, it challenges us to reflect on our own decisive moment.

Notes

[1] Spencer Johnson, *Who Moved My Cheese?* (NY: G.P. Putnam's Sons, 1998). Spencer Johnson (1938–2017), a medical physician, wrote the book to help patients who were mired in their own fear of change and stayed stuck in repetitive cycles. The book maintained an extraordinary run on bestseller lists, including over 200 weeks on the *Publishers Weekly* and five years on *The New York Times* bestseller list. *Time* magazine called the book "the bestselling business book of all time." Andrea Sachs, "Who Moved My Cheese? (1998), By Spencer Johnson," *Time* (August 9, 2011). The success of *Who Moved My Cheese?* led to a proliferation of sequels, including *Out of the Maze, I Moved Your Cheese, Who Cut the Cheese* and *We Move Our Own Cheese!*

[2] Ron Charles, "Today is the 20th Anniversary of 'Who Moved My Cheese?' Why Does It Still Move Us?" *Washington Post* (September 6, 2018), E1. Describing it as "the consummate American self-help book," historian Mitch Horowitz notes that *Who Moved My Cheese?* possesses a key trait of the genre: "a religious inflection or [is] written, however subtly, from a perspective of faith."

[3] James Morone, *Hellfire Nation: The Politics of Sin in American History* (New Haven: Yale University Press,

2003), 381. Morone argues that religious and moral fervor drives America's political life. In post-World War II America, Christianity became deeply intertwined with the Cold War, defending the American way of life and government against the evils of communism. Political leaders framed America as a God-fearing nation versus communist regimes led by the former Soviet Union, or the "evil empire," a term later popularized by Ronald Reagan.

[4] Robert Ellwood, *The Fifties Spiritual Marketplace: American Religion in a Decade of Conflict* (New Brunswick, NJ: Rutgers Univ. Press, 1997), 5. Ellwood contends that Christianity flourished during the 1950s due to the vast array of denominations and styles that emerged in the new suburbs. He argues that this unprecedented growth was not as a response to a spiritual revival, but rather a social and political current that swept the public toward a religious outlook.

[5] Ibid., 7.

[6] Ibid., 6. Ellwood argues that church growth driven largely by competition and choice, noting that "the crux of this 'new paradigm'" is the realization that "organized religion thrives in the United States in an open-market system."

[7] "How Religious Are Americans?" *Gallup* (March 29, 2024), https://news.gallup.com/poll/358364/religious-

americans.aspx. Today, about 22% to 24% of US adults identify as "nones"—a stark contrast to the 1950s, when nearly 0% reported having no religious preference.

[8] Will Herberg, *Protestant—Catholic—Jew* (NY: Doubleday, 1955), 260. Herberg adds, "It is thus frequent a religiousness without serious commitment, without real inner conviction, without genuine existential decision. What should reach down to the core of existence, shattering and renewing, merely skims the surface of life, and yet succeeds in generating the sincere feeling of being religious. Religion thus becomes a kind of protection the self throws up against the radical demand of faith." Ibid.

[9] Jim Dueck, *Then, Now, and Why Now: Sixty Years of Change in Education* (Lanham, MD: Rowman & Littlefield), 75. "On a typical Sunday morning in the period from 1955-58, almost half of all Americans were attending church—the highest percentage in U.S. history." Dueck uses the unprecedented growth to illustrate how religion served as a central social institution that anchored American life.

[10] Jeffrey Jones, "Church Attendance Has Declined in Most U.S. Religious Groups," *Gallup* (March 25, 2024), https://news.gallup.com/poll/642548/church-attendance-declined-religious-groups.aspx. The report identifies two primary drivers for the decline: increasing secularization and a lack of religious upbringing among younger generations.

[11] Lovett Weems, "The Coming Death Tsunami," *Ministry Matters* (October 5, 2011), https://ministrymatters.com/2011-10-05_the_coming_death_tsunami/. Weems explains the dilemma of many struggling churches: "A church then gets to a point at which attendance has declined so much that making the budget each year becomes the preoccupation of the church and its leadership. Each year they search for that one new source of income or cut in spending so they can manage to make their plan. They also realize that even these yearly heroic efforts will not be enough going forward as they note the high percentage of their annual giving that no comes from those over age 70."

[12] Kevin Singer and Josh Packard, "Trust in Religious Institutions Is Low Among Gen Z—But Young People Are Keeping the Faith in Other Ways," *Religion in Public* (February 19, 2021), https://religioninpublic.blog/2021/02/19/trust-in-religious-institutions-is-low-among-gen-z-but-young-people-are-keeping-the-faith-in-other-ways/. "Remarkably, this suggest that more than half of young people who claim a religious affiliation have little trust in the very religious institutions with which they identify."

[13] Jeffrey Jones, "Church Attendance Has Declined in Most U.S. Religious Groups."

[14] "Historic Ohio Church to Close After 220 Years of Continual Service," *Local12 News* (April 15, 2025), www.youtube.com/watch?v=ZblFYWUYw5E. Founded in 1803, Elizabethtown United Methodist Church, was the "oldest institution of any kind in the greater Cincinnati area" before it closed. According to Simpson, "We don't know of anything else that's been in continuous existence that long."

[15] The Greek word for *rekindle* in 2 Timothy 1:6 is ἀναζωπυρέω (*anazōpureō*). Strong's number: G0329.

[16] See K. Kale Yu, *Freestyle: Evangelism as Expressing Jesus* (Greensboro, NC: Elmore Townes, 2025). Most outreach and evangelistic efforts focus on a program; freestyle, however, focuses on the individual. "Freestyle is an individualized, custom-made platform designed by the individual to release Jesus. Freestyle appeals to the postmodern mind by having 'my truth' as the epicenter of the individual's evangelistic expression" (p. 15). Freestyle avoids the postmodern perception of faith as being forced upon the individual by elevating the individual over institutional programming. This approach circumvents contemporary skepticism and resistance by grounding the spiritual experience in personal agency rather than external imposition.

[17] Ryan Burge, "My Church Is Closing, and I Don't Know What Comes Next—for Me, or America," *Deseret News* (July

25, 2024), www.deseret.com/faith/2024/07/25/ryan-burge-church-closing-the-nones/. The situation is "hollowing out" the religious middle—those who attend church once or twice a month. The loss of these voices has created a religious all-or-nothing landscape. As churchgoers drift toward either the devout core or the "nones," moderate congregations are left without a vital pipeline of new members.

[18] Ibid.

[19] Derrek Belase, "A Church Closing That Hits Home," *UM News* (November 10, 2022), www.umnews.org/en/news/a-church-closing-that-hits-home. Looking back on how the church shaped his faith, Belase realized that the "main thing" he learned was the depth of Jesus's love. For him, that love was most tangibly demonstrated through the fellow believers who "showed me his love" through the years.

[20] Ibid. Belase provided examples of the can-do spirit of past church members. "The Great Depression throw the church another curveball. Rising to the occasion as they always do, the women of the church raised money by serving plate lunches to the local Rotary Club. They started this project Dec. 7, 1938, and continued the tradition for the next 82 years without interruption. Another very unique fundraiser was the annual 'Calendar Supper.' Started in 1935 to finance the youth activities, 12 tables

were festooned with decorations depicting each of the 12 months. Participants sat at the table of their birth month, and a rousing auction would take place after the fellowship supper." Chapter 3, "The You-Do-It Challenge," explores the premise that contemporary church renewal depends on a you-do-it spirit.

[21] Ibid. Belase concludes this poignant reflection with a note of resilient hope: "May the seeds planted during the Carnegie church's 118-year history continue to bear much fruit."

[22] Ryan Burge, "My Church Is Closing, and I Don't Know What Comes Next—for Me, or America."

[23] Ibid.

[24] Ellen Rose, "As Hundreds of Churches Sit Empty, Some Become Hotels and Restaurants," *The New York Times* (August 4, 2024), www.nytimes.com/2024/08/04/business/church-development-reuse.html. A sociologist and Presbyterian minister, Lindner edited the *Yearbook of American and Canadian Churches*. Lindner noted that this figure, which could approach 20 percent of all Protestant churches, has grown significantly over the past decade.

[25] Scott Neuman, "The Faith See Both Crisis and Opportunity as Churches Close Across the Country," NPR

(May 17, 2023), www.npr.org/2023/05/17/1175452002/church-closings-religious-affiliation. The article explores the church's role as a vital social safety net, suggesting that its disappearance leaves a big void in community support. Concerns are expressed "about how the U.S. will cope with the sudden evaporation of community services that churches once provided—food banks, help for troubled teens, addiction treatment and other programs." While many European societies maintain state-funded support system, the U.S. has historically relied on religious and community institutions to provide that social safety net. "So, when those services [from churches] disappear, there really isn't anything to replace them."

[26] Ibid.

[27] Aaron Zitner, "America Pulls Back From Values That Once Defined It, WSJ-NORC Poll Finds," *The Wall Street Journal* (March 27, 2023), www.wsj.com/articles/americans-pull-back-from-values-that-once-defined-u-s-wsj-norc-poll-finds-df8534cd?mod=hp_lead_pos10. "The share of Americans who say that having children, involvement in their community and hard work are very important values has also fallen. Tolerance for others, deemed very important by 80% of Americans as recently as four years ago, has fallen to 58% since then."

[28] Ibid. McInturff explained that "perhaps the toll of our political division, Covid and the lowest economic confidence in decades is having a startling effect on our core values."

[29] Jeffrey Jones, "U.S. Church Membership Falls Below Majority for First Time," *Gallup* (March 29, 2021), https://news.gallup.com/poll/341963/church-membership-falls-below-majority-first-time.aspx. "Church membership is strongly correlated with age, as 66% of traditionalists—U.S. adults born before 1946—belong to a church compared with 58% of baby boomers, 50% of those in Generation X and 36% of millennials. The limited data Gallup has on church membership among the portion of Generation Z that has reached adulthood are so far showing church membership rates similar to those for millennials."

[30] Ibid.

[31] Kate Quinones, "Burned-Out Pastor Builds Global Mental Health Resources for Churches," *EWTN News* (October 27, 2025), www.denvercatholic.org/burned-out-pastor-builds-global-mental-health-resources-for-churches. Thinking back at his burnout experience "was really confusing," according to Whitehead. "I didn't have language, or self-permission, or a framework to really understand what I was going through," he said. "But how I

would describe it was a feeling of fear, anxiety, and feeling trapped."

[32] Michael Woolf, "Burned Out, Exhausted, Leaving: A New Survey Finds Clergy Are Not Ok," *Religion News Service* (January 25, 2024), https://religionnews.com/2024/01/25/burned-out-exhausted-leaving-a-new-survey-finds-clergy-are-not-ok/.

[33] "38% of U.S. Pastors Have Thought About Quitting Full-Time Ministry in the Past Year," *Barna* (November 16, 2021), www.barna.com/research/pastors-well-being/. To address the burnout crisis, Barna researchers suggest that "keeping the right younger leaders encouraged and in their ministry roles will be crucial" to the vitality of US congregations over the next decade."

[34] Cited in "5 Shocking Realities About the Real State of Pastor Burnout," *Western North Carolina Conference* (April 12, 2023), www.wnccumc.org/resourcedetail/5-shocking-realities-about-the-real-state-of-pastor-burnout-17392915. Pastor burnout has reached a "five-alarm fire" level, severely eroding the confidence of clergy. "In 2015, 66% of pastors said they felt more confident in their calling into ministry than they did when they first entered ministry. Today, only 35% of pastors say they feel more confident in their calling than when they started."

[35] Ibid.

[36] Tish H. Warren, "Why Pastors Are Burning Out," *The New York Times* (August 28, 2022), www.nytimes.com/2022/08/28/opinion/pastor-burnout-pandemic.html. Clergy must navigate a precarious landscape fraught with political landmines, yet remain "charged with the task of continuing to love and care for even those within their church who disagree with them vehemently and vocally."

[37] Ibid.

[38] Benedict Vigers and Julie Ray, "Drop in U.S. Religiosity Among Largest in World," *Gallup* (November 13, 2025), https://news.gallup.com/poll/697676/drop-religiosity-among-largest-world.aspx. "About half of Americans now say religion is *not* an important part of their daily life [emphasis mine]."

[39] Ibid.

[40] Prashansa Gadgil, "Merriam-Webster's Word for 2023 Is Out—Any Guesses?" *Medium* (November 28, 2023), https://medium.com/illumination-curated/merriam-websters-word-for-2023-is-out-any-guesses-d4d5a5f6fc31. Also, see "Word of the Year 2023," *Merriam-Webster*, www.merriam-webster.com/wordplay/word-of-the-year-2023. In "Word of the Year 2023," Merriam-

Webster explains how the term is distorted in modern contexts by content creators. "Ironically, with 'authentic content creators' now recognized as the gold standard for building trust, 'authenticity' has become a performance."

[41] Jule Hubbard, "Eshcol Church Latest Methodist Closing," *Wilkes Journal-Patriot* (July 24, 2015), https://www.journalpatriot.com/news/eshcol-church-latest-methodist-closing/article_f87831ac-322e-11e5-b631-f73a2b4a3303.html.

[42] Eric Sentell, "100,000 U.S. Churches May Close by 2050. What Can Be Done?" *Medium* (February 12, 2025), https://medium.com/backyard-theology/100-000-u-s-churches-may-close-by-2050-what-can-be-done-11242ca0df6d. According to Sentell, the church is losing young people because it prioritizes the initial decision to follow Jesus while neglecting the long-term work of discipleship. "Being 'seeker-friendly' became the goal for most U.S. churches: attract and retain non-Christians with entertaining services, rocking worship music, and fun-filled activities for the kids. Discipling people into Christ-likeness became an after-thought, as thought it happens by osmosis. Because Millennials and Gen Z lacked discipleship in the 1980s, 1990s, and 2000s, they became adults in the 2010s and 2020s who were more likely than previous generations to leave church. Many simply lacked

deep conviction in their faith and connection to their church communities."

[43] Casey Diaz, "I Marked People for Death. Jesus Marked Me for Life," *Christianity Today* (May 2019), www.christianitytoday.com/2019/04/casey-diaz-shot-caller-marked-people-death-gang-leader/.

[44] Ibid.

[45] Ibid.

[46] Mark Ellis, "God Played a Video of His Life On Prison Cell Wall," *GodReports* (September 30, 2019), www.godreports.com/2019/09/god-played-a-video-of-his-life-on-prison-cell-wall/.

[47] Ibid.

[48] Casey Diaz, *The Shot Caller: A Latino Gangbanger's Miraculous Escape from a Life of Violence to a New Life in Christ* (Nashville, TN: Thomas Nelson, 2019). The book is also available in both ebook and audiobook formats.

[49] For more information on Casey Diaz's *The Shot Call Podcast*, see https://creators.spotify.com/pod/profile/theshotcaller/. To book Casey Diaz as a speaker, go to https://caseydiaz.net/contact/.

50 Lucy Blaylock, "Lucy's Love Blankets," *The Christian Heart* (September 21, 2020), https://thechristianheart.com/lucys-love-blankets/.

51 To donate to Lucy's nonprofit, go to her Facebook page: www.facebook.com/lucysloveblankets/.

52 Lee Wing-Sze, "MC Jin, Re-Branded," *South China Morning Post* (March 3, 2013), www.scmp.com/lifestyle/arts-culture/article/1166585/mc-jin-re-branded.

53 Nicola Menzie, "Evolution of Jin: Former Ruff Ryder's Fall to Grace," *The Christian Post* (February 9, 2013), www.christianpost.com/news/evolution-of-jin-former-ruff-ryders-fall-to-grace.html.

54 Edward Shih, "Chinese-American Rapper MC Jin Testifies to God's Blessings in His Life," *The Gospel Herald* (May 17, 2011), www.gospelherald.com/news/chinese-american-rapper-mc-jin-testifies-to-gods-blessings-in-his-life.

55 Lee Wing-Sze, "MC Jin, Re-Branded."

56 Ibid.

57 "Dorothea Dix Begins Her Crusade," *MassMoments* (March 28, 1841), www.massmoments.org/moment-details/dorothea-dix-begins-her-crusade.html.

[58] Shawn Logan, "Dorothea Dix: Crusader for the Insane," *Kentucky Historic Institutions* (July 26, 2017), https://kyhi.org/2017/07/26/dorothea-dix-crusader-for-the-insane/.

[59] Mark Ellis, "God Played a Video of His Life On Prison Cell Wall." Diaz describes Frances Procter as a "diminutive African American woman."

[60] Ibid.

[61] Lillian Kwon, "10 Questions for Pastor Mark Batterson," *Christian Post* (October 29, 2009), www.christianpost.com/news/theater-church-pastor.html.

[62] Casey Diaz, "Ex-Prisoner Urges Christians to Remember Those in Jail at Christmastime," *Christian Post* (December 25, 2019), www.christianpost.com/voices/ex-prisoner-urges-christians-to-remember-those-in-jail-at-christmastime.html.

[63] Mark Ellis, "God Played a Video of His Life on Prison Cell Wall."

[64] Casey Diaz, "Ex-Prisoner Urges Christians to Remember Those in Jail at Christmastime."

[65] Mark Ellis, "God Played a Video of His Life on Prison Cell Wall."

66 Daniel Hofkamp, "Bible Stories in LEGO: The Passion of Christ Comes to Life in Stop Motion," *Evangelical Focus* (April 16, 2025), https://evangelicalfocus.com/life-tech/30839/bible-stories-in-lego-the-passion-of-christ-comes-to-life-in-stop-motion. All content produced by Whitehouse's Go Chatter Studios is free on their website and YouTube channel. Go to https://gochatterstudios.org and www.youtube.com/@GoChatterStudios. To reach a global audience, their animations are translated into multiple languages.

67 Devyn Lyon, "Collinsville Girl Helps Create 'Blessing Boxes' To Give Back to Her Community," FOX23 (May 17, 2024), www.fox23.com/news/collinsville-girl-helps-create-blessing-boxes-to-give-back-to-her-community/article_9fafc7be-1489-11ef-9803-1f06d0e4d5ce.html.

68 Ibid.

69 "Feeding an ARMY of 2200 HUNGRY Japanese Students for Lunch," *Japanese Food Craftsman* (July 6, 2025), www.youtube.com/watch?v=gBHZxcQcYgg.

70 The findings are cited in Alison Meyer, "How Gen Z Is Shaping a New Era of Mental-Health Care," *MSU Denver* (September 30, 2024), https://red.msudenver.edu/2024/how-gen-z-is-shaping-a-new-era-of-mental-health-

care/#:~:text=Dubbed%20the%20%E2%80%9CAnxious%2
0Generation%2C%E2%80%9D,options%20in%20partnersh
ip%20with%20UWill. Older generations may be surprised
by Gen Z's openness regarding mental health. "Gen Zers
are also more open about their struggles and more
proactive in seeking help. Two of every five Gen Zers
regularly attend therapy, and 53% have sought
professional mental-health services at some point,
according to Harmony Healthcare IT. In fact, 87% report
feeling comfortable discussing mental health, and over
60% feel comfortable sharing their struggles."

[71] Lindsey Tanner, "CDC Data Shows U.S. Teen Girls 'In
Crisis' With Unprecedented Rise in Suicidal Behavior," *PBS
Newshour* (February 13, 2023),
www.pbs.org/newshour/health/cdc-data-shows-u-s-
teen-girls-in-crisis-with-unprecedented-rise-in-suicidal-
behavior#:~:text=More%20than%2017%2C000%20U.S.%2
0high,Indian%20and%20Alaska%20Native%20youth.
Recent global and societal events are converged to
exacerbate the mental health crisis among young people.
"Isolation, online schooling, and increased reliance on
social media during the pandemic made things worse for
many kids."

[72] "U.S. Teen Girls Experiencing Increased Sadness and
Violence," CDC (February 13, 2023),
www.cdc.gov/media/releases/2023/p0213-yrbs.html.

Debra Houry, CDC's Chief Medical Officer, said, "High school should be a time for trailblazing, not trauma. Proven school prevention program can offer teens a vital lifeline in these growing waves of trauma."

[73] Vani Sanganeria, "Students Become Lifeline for Peers Facing Suspensions, Mental Health Struggles," *EdSource* (February 10, 2026), https://edsource.org/2026/mental-health-peer-counseling/750829#:~:text=Peer%2Dto%2Dpeer%20support%20has,funds%20to%20expand%20its%20capacity.

[74] Laura Ziegler, "'It's Literally Life-Saving.' Kansas Teens Support Each Other Through Mental Health Struggles," KCUR (December 5, 2022), www.kcur.org/news/2022-12-05/its-literally-life-saving-kansas-teens-support-each-other-through-mental-health-struggles.

[75] Brooke Knoop, "What People Get Wrong About Leaving Institutional Church [Episode 22]," *reChurch Podcast* (November 25, 2025), 9:53–10:35, www.youtube.com/watch?v=JeUNfRhV5hg. Brooke Knoop is the co-host of the *reChurch* podcast. To listen to the podcast, go to https://rechurchpodcast.buzzsprout.com/.

[76] Quoted in Clare Ansberry, "Why Middle-Aged Americans Aren't Going Back to Church," *The Wall Street Journal* (August 1, 2023), www.wsj.com/articles/church-

attendance-religion-generation-x-6ee5f11d?mod=hp_featst_pos3. Contrary to assumptions, "church attendance for Gen Xers [the generation that follows baby boomers] has dropped off more dramatically than other age groups." According to George Barna, "No generation endured greater spiritual turbulence than Gen X during the pandemic."

77 See Josh Packard and Ashleigh Hope, *Church Refugees: Sociologists Reveals Why People Are Done But Not Their Faith* (Loveland, CO: Group Publishing, 2015), 79. While many are familiar with the "nones"—those with no religious affiliation—a newer category has emerged: the "dones." This term refers to formerly active and faithful church leaders who have made the deliberate choice to leave.

78 Ibid., 61.

79 Clare Ansberry, "Why Middle-Aged Americans Aren't Going Back to Church."

80 Spencer Johnson, *Who Moved My Cheese?*, 70.

81 Ibid., 41.

82 Ibid., 65.

226